2020

Keto Diabetic & Egg Free Cookbook

Egg Free and Dairy Free Ketogenic Diet for Allergy, Diabetes, Cholesterol Management and Effective Weight Loss (Egg free, Dairy free, Gluten free, Low Cholesterol, Whole, Grain free, Sugar free, Paleo).

Jenny Pale

2020 Keto Diabetic & Egg Free Cookbook

Copyright © 2019 by Pale

All rights reserved. This book or any portion thereof may not be reproduced or used in any manner whatsoever without the express written permission of the publisher except for the use of brief quotations in a book review. The scanning, uploading, and distribution of this book via the Internet or via any other means without the permission of the publisher is illegal and punishable by law.

Please purchase only authorized editions of this book and don't participate in or encourage electronic piracy of copyrighted materials. If you would like to share this book with another person, please purchase an additional copy for each person you share it with, or ask them to buy their own copies. This was hard work for the author and he appreciates it.

Table of Contents

TABLE OF CONTENTS 2

INTRODUCTION 9

CHAPTER ONE: INTRODUCTION TO KETO 10

What is the Ketogenic Diet? 10

Why go Keto? 10

Losing Weight with the Ketogenic Diet? 11

What Is the Difference Between Dairy-Free Keto and Paleo? 13

Benefits of Diary-Free Keto 13

Diary-Free Keto Friendly Ingredients in Your Pantry 15

Cooking Equipment 16

Swap It Out! 18

Foods You Should Consume More 18

Food You Should Consume in Moderation 20

Foods to Avoid 21

CHAPTER TWO: BREAKFAST 23

Hot Chicken and Waffles 23

Sausage Gravy 24

Iced Green Tea Latte 26

Cherry Almond Breakfast Shake 27

French Toast Cereal 28

Sausage Breakfast Hash 29

Truffle Keto Cheesecake 30

Radish Hash Browns with Onion and Green Pepper 32

Perfect Bacon 33

Keto Faux Cappuccino 34

Cauliflower Oatmeal with Blueberries 35

CHAPTER THREE: STAPLES, SAUCES & DRESSINGS 36

Red Pepper Dry Rub 36

Everything Marinade 37

Lemon-Garlic Dressing 38

Pico De Gallo 39

Guacamole 40

Tartar Sauce 41

Pickled Cucumbers and Onions 42

Herb-Kale Pesto 43

Cream Cheese Icing 44

Chocolate Sauce 45

CHAPTER FOUR: SMALL BITES, SMOOTHIES AND DRINKS 46

Spinach-Blueberry Smoothie 46

Low-carb ginger smoothie 47

Virgin Strawberry Margarita 48

Chocolate Sauce 49

Creamy Cinnamon Smoothie 50

Lemon-Cashew Smoothie 51

Shrimp Cocktail 52

Pico De Gallo 53

Citrus Avocado Salsa 54

Herbed Balsamic Dressing 55

Virgin Strawberry Margarita 56

Spiced-Chocolate Fat Bombs 57

CHAPTER FIVE: SEA FOODS 58

Fried Oysters in The Oven 58

Tuna with Greens and Blueberries 59

Coconut Shrimp 60

Bacon-Wrapped Scallop Cups 61

Salmon Patties 62

Country Club Crab Cakes 63

Shrimp Sti-fry 64

Baked Salmon with Lemon and Mush 65

Pan-fried Soft Shell Crab 67

Mussels with Lemon-Garlic Sauce and Parsley 68

Three-Minute Lobster Tail 69

CHAPTER SIX: SOUPS AND SALADS 70

Cauliflower and Bacon Soup 70

Hearty Vegetable Soup 72

Pizza Soup 73

Stuffed-Pepper Soup 75

Broccoli Salad 76

Chilled Tomato and Ham Soup 77

Chinese Beef and Broccoli Soup 78

Turkey and Orzo Soup 80

Coconut Ginger Chicken Soup 81

Manhattan Clam Chowder 83

Wedge Salad with Ranch Dressing 85

Cold Cauliflower "Pasta" Salad 86

Smoky Spicy Chicken Stew 87

Simple Ham Salad 89

Thai Red Curry Shrimp Soup 90

Chicken Salad with Grapes and Almonds 92

Ham and Fauxtato Soup 93

Salmon Soup 94

Spicy Shrimp Salad 96

CHAPTER SEVEN: POULTRY RECIPES 97

Slow-Cooker Buffalo Chicken 97

Salt-And-Pepper Chicken Kebabs with Pineapple 98

Umami Chicken Burgers 99

Best Fried Chicken Ever 100

Chicken and Asparagus Curry 101

Chicken Tinga 103

Guacamole Lovers' Stuffed Chicken 105

Chicken Meatball Marinara with Bean Sprouts and Broccoli 107

Garlic Chicken Wings 108

Black Skillet Chicken Thighs with Artichoke Hearts 109

Sheet Pan BBQ Chicken Breasts 110

Chicken with Dried Beef 111

Chili-Garlic Chicken with Broccoli 112

Poppy Seed Chicken 113

Curry Braised Chicken Legs 114

Turkey Rissoles 116

Chicken and Mushroom Kabobs 117

Easy Asian Chicken Legs 119

Lemon Pepper Chicken Tender 121

Paprika Chicken 123

Bundt Pan Chicken 125

Coconut Chicken 127

CHAPTER EIGHT: BEEF & PORK RECIPES 129

Dinner Roast with Vegetables 129

Beef Liver Burgers 130

Easy BBQ Brisket 131

Lamb Chops With Kalamata Tapenade 133

Rosemary-Garlic Lamb Racks 135

Philly Cheeses Teak Bake 136

Secret Seasoning Sirloin Steak 138

Slopy Joes 139

Curry Short Ribs 140

Lamb Leg with Sun-Dried Tomato Pesto 142

Fajita Kabobs 144

Cabbage Slaw with Ground Beef 146

Bacon-Wrapped Beef Tenderloin 147

Cheese Burger Hash 148

Kielbasa and Sauerkraut 150

Potluck BBQ Pork 151

Garlic Pork Chops with Onion-And-Mushroom Gravy 152

Lemon-Garlic Pork Tenderloin with Radishes and Green Pepper 154

Citrus Pork Shoulder with Spicy Cilantro Ginger Sauce 155

Dry Rub Ribs 158

Bacon-Wrapped "Fried" Pickles 159

Stuffed Poblano Peppers 160

Shepherd's Pie 161

Ground-Pork Skillet With Zucchini And Onion 162

Sausage Balls 163

CHAPTER EIGHT: DESSERTS 164

No-Bake Haystack Cookies 164

Macadami Nut Butter Cups 165

Chocolate Chip Skillet Cookie 166

Chocolate Bacon With Pink Hi-Malayan Salt 167

CONCLUSION 168

Introduction

A ketogenic diet is a way of eating that is very low in carbohydrates. Reducing carbs changes the body's metabolism and is perfect for easy weight loss. The metabolic process burns fat when it doesn't have enough carbohydrates.

The first question I get about the Keto diet is the "What if I don't eat (food allergy or food aversion)" questions. What if I don't eat eggs? What if I don't eat gluten? What if I don't eat dairy? Can I still do Keto? Yes, you can! But allergens, rightfully so, are at the forefront of people's minds when they start a new diet. I try to help as much as possible but I don't have the experience or extensive research to help every single person out.

I understand this struggle very well because I am dairy-free and gluten-free. So many recipes I have found in the keto diet are packed with heavy cream and cheese so finding recipes that fit my needs were a struggle.

Not including dairy from your diet can be an effective way to speed up your weight loss and help reversing type 2 diabetes. Dairy products contain not only milk sugar (lactose), but also milk protein (casein), which stimulates insulin secretion more than other types of protein.

In addition, following the Ketogenic diet can minimize your dependent on Insulin and medication requirements thereby reducing the cost of caring for diabetes and potential side effects from drugs.

In over 20 studies, Keto diets resulted in greater weight loss and improvements of cholesterol levels thereby lowering your risk of developing heart disease. To ensure the recipes in this book complies with improving the cholestorol level of your body, high cholesterol content ingredients such as Egg and butter has been eliminated from the recipes.

This book serves as a beginners guide to the ketogenic diet, Dairy & Egg free Keto. It contains over 150 Dairy free, Egg free and Gluten free Ketogenic recipes for Allergies and Weight loss.

Chapter One: Introduction to Keto

What is the Ketogenic Diet?

A ketogenic diet is a way of eating that is very low in carbohydrates. Reducing carbs changes the body's metabolism and is perfect for easy weight loss. The metabolic process burns fat when it doesn't have enough carbohydrates. There are, however, many more important benefits. The ketogenic diet limits the amounts of grains, starches and sugars that are consumed and fuels your body with fat. This reduced insulin levels and lets fat burn much more efficiently. In a 2003 study, participants using a ketogenic diet lost more than twice the weight than participants that restricted calories. One of the reasons for this rapid weight loss is that the ketogenic diet replicates the state of fasting. A fasting person burns fat, and the ketogenic diet derives its energy primarily from burned fat. The typical ketogenic diet gets 70 percent of calories from fat, 20 percent of calories from protein, and 5 percent of calories from carbohydrates.

Why go Keto?

When you eat a ketogenic diet, your body becomes efficient at burning fat for fuel. This is great for a multitude of reasons, not the least of which is that fat contains more than double the calories of most carbs, so you need to eat far less food by weight every day. Your body more readily burns the fat it has stored (the fat you're trying to get rid of), resulting in more weight loss. Using fat for fuel provides consistent energy levels, and it does not spike your blood glucose, so you don't experience the highs and lows when eating large amounts of carbs. Consistent energy levels throughout your day means you can get more done and feel less tired doing so.

In addition to those benefits, eating a keto diet in the long term has been proven to:

- Result in more weight loss (specifically body fat)
- Reduce blood sugar and insulin resistance (commonly reversing prediabetes and type 2 diabetes)
- Reduce triglyceride levels
- Reduce blood pressure
- Improve levels of HDL (good) and LDL (bad) cholesterol
- Improve brain function

Losing Weight with the Ketogenic Diet?

The following tips should be applied while losing weight through the ketogenic diet plan:

1. **Choose a diet containing fewer carbohydrates**

You need to cut down on your consumption of starch and sugar. This idea is more than a century old. There have been a lot of diet plans which are based on reducing the amount of carbs you take. The new thing with the Ketogenic diet is that you provide your body with an alternate source of energy to depend on, which is fats. When you do not eat carbohydrates or eat them moderately, your body is capable of burning 300 additional calories per day, even when you are resting! It means that this amount of burnt calories is equal to a gym session of moderate physical activity.

2. **Eat when you feel hungry**

You do not need to stay hungry all the time to lose weight. This is the most common mistake committed by people who start a low carb diet. In the Ketogenic diet, you do not have to be scared of fats. Carbohydrates and fats are two major sources of energy for our body. If you are snatching carbs from your body, you need to give it an ample supply of fats. Low fats and low carbs equal to starvation, and we do not want that, do we? Starvation results in cravings and fatigue. That is why, people who starve give up easily on their diet plans. The better solution is to consume natural fat till the time you are satisfied. Some of the natural fats are full fat cream, butter, olive oil, meat, bacon, fatty fish, coconut oil, eggs.

3. **Eat real food**

This is one more common mistake made by Ketogenic followers that they get fooled by the fraudulent but creative marketing of "low-carb" foods. A real Ketogenic diet should be supported by real food. It implies the food which is being eaten by humans for millions of years. For example, fish, meat, vegetables, olive oil, butter, nuts, etc.

4. **Eat only if you feel hungry**

You must have read tip number 2 above. In the Ketogenic diet, eat when you are hungry. Do not eat when you are not feeling hungry. Let us elaborate why we are stressing this point again. Unnecessary snacking may become a mammoth issue in the Ketogenic diet. Some products are just so easily available, and they are so tempting that you cannot resist them.

5. **You can skip meals**

Yes, you heard it right. You can even skip breakfast if you are not feeling hungry. This holds truth for any meal. When you are strictly following the Ketogenic diet, your hunger goes down significantly, especially if you have to lose a lot of weight. Your body is happily busy in burning excess fats and reduces your temptation to eat.

6. **Wisely measure your development**

Losing weight successfully might get trickier sometimes. If you focus on your weight all the time and step on the weighing scale all the time, you may get mislead. It de-motivates you and makes you anxious needlessly.

7. **Be persistent**

You would have all those chunks of fats around your waist and thighs in several years. So, how do you expect to lose all the extra fat in just a few weeks? If you want to shed that extra weight permanently, you have to make persistent efforts.

What Is the Difference Between Dairy-Free Keto and Paleo?

The paleo diet is an eating plan based on what prehistoric humans might have eaten. It eliminates grains, legumes, processed sugar, and most dairy sources, but lets you eat meats, eggs, nuts and seeds, fruits, vegetables, unrefined fats and oils, and natural sweeteners (such as maple syrup and honey). Although it is relatively low-carb, it does not restrict carbohydrates to the same degree as the keto diet, and therefore does not engage ketosis. The keto diet, on the other hand, focuses primarily on the three macronutrients of fat, protein, and carbohydrates. By consuming a lot of fat but not very much protein and very few carbs, someone on the keto diet can induce ketosis, a metabolic state in which the body burns fat instead of carbohydrates for energy. The big, shiny difference between the two is ketosis—teaching your body to keep burning fat—and that is what we're after.

Benefits of Diary-Free Keto

People choose to go dairy-free for a number of reasons. Perhaps the most common is lactose intolerance (the inability to digest lactose, the sugar found in milk)—which 65 percent of people in the world have, according to the National Institutes of Health. There are a host of additional medical conditions and symptoms that can be negatively impacted by dairy consumption, and it's important to check in with your health and assess whether eliminating dairy might help you achieve your specific desires and goals. If you have any of the following conditions, consider whether dairy-free might be the right modifier for your keto diet. It certainly was for me.

Stomach Pain: When stomach pain results from food sensitivities, it can be difficult to pinpoint the problem. An elimination diet can be helpful, and often, the problem turns out to be dairy products. In my case, my stomach was often hurting and uneasy, even after I had adapted to the keto diet. Once I went dairy-free, the problem was solved.

Severe Bloating: The inability to break down lactose can lead to major digestive problems, including gas and bloating. For those already prone to inflammation, dairy can aggravate the symptoms.

Constipation: Many people prone to constipation are sensitive to certain ingredients, dairy being one of them.

Gut Health: The impact of dietary changes on the human microbiome (the trillions of bacteria, viruses, and fungi that make up much of the body) is a constantly expanding area of science. According to the T.H. Chan School of Public

Health at Harvard University, certain dietary influences can cause a disturbance in the balance of coexisting microbiota in the body. It wasn't until dairy-free keto helped me heal my gut that I even realized this was the root of so many of my issues.

Lactose Intolerance: If you've been holding back from keto because you're lactose intolerant and it seems to involve so much butter and cheese, worry no more! You don't have to eat dairy to eat keto, and you can still reap all the benefits. It's also worth noting that many people are lactose intolerant and don't realize it; in fact, many of the symptoms listed on this page can often be traced back to an absence of lactase, the enzyme that breaks down lactose. If you have even mild issues with certain dairy products, it's something to consider.

Stalled Weight Loss: If you feel like you're doing everything right and still can't get past that stubborn weight-loss plateau, try eliminating dairy. It might just be exactly what your body needs—either because of the conditions named above, such as bloating and lactose intolerance, or simply because it will change your caloric intake.

Polycystic Ovary Syndrome (PCOS): According to the U.S. Department of Health and Human Services, PCOS is "one of the most common endocrine disorders among women of reproductive age." Although current studies are inconclusive, it's possible that PCOS symptoms can be aggravated by dairy intake. Further research is needed to draw firm conclusions, but the anecdotal evidence was enough to convince me it was worth a try—and now I can add my own story to that list.

Irritable Bowel Syndrome (IBS): Most people with IBS are lactose intolerant, so keeping your diet dairy-free will help alleviate IBS symptoms and aid with stomach comfort.

Diary-Free Keto Friendly Ingredients in Your Pantry

- Almond flour
- Alternative sweeteners, such as Swerve (granulated and confectioners')
- Baking powder
- Bone broth
- Cayenne Coconut flour
- Coconut milk, canned
- Coconut, shredded
- Grapeseed oil
- Olive oil Pepper, black
- Salt, such as Himalayan pink salt, which is loaded with minerals and trace nutrients; I use it on everything
- Vanilla extract, alcohol-free

Refrigerated Essentials

- Bacon Barbecue sauce, sugar-free, low-carb (such as Tessemae's brand)
- Broccoli
- Cauliflower
- Cream cheese, dairy-free (such as Kite Hill brand)
- Eggs
- Ketchup, sugar-free, low-carb (such as Primal Kitchen brand)
- Marinades, sugar-free, low-carb
- Mayonnaise, sugar-free, low-carb (such as Primal Kitchen brand)
- Meats, grass-fed
- Mustard, sugar-free, low-carb (such as Primal Kitchen brand)

- Pickles
- Plain yogurt, dairy-free (such as Kite Hill brand)
- Salami, sugar-free, low-carb
- Other vegetables and greens

Other Perishable Essentials

- Avocados
- Garlic
- Lemons
- Onions
- Tomatoes

The Deal with Ghee

Many people wonder if ghee, or clarified butter, is the exception to the dairy-free rule. I will not be using ghee throughout this book in order to keep it 100 percent dairy-free, but some people with lactose intolerance are able to tolerate ghee, as it has very low levels of lactose and is thus unlikely to cause a reaction. However, you should always know and understand your own tolerance levels and dietary preferences. For those who can and do use ghee, feel free to replace the oils in my recipes with equal amounts of ghee.

Cooking Equipment

To cook the recipe in this book. You don't necessarily need a bunch of fancy equipment in your kitchen. These are few key items you should have in your kitchen.

Cutting Board: Because you'll be cutting, dicing, and mincing fresh ingredients, you need a proper surface for safe and handy chopping.

Cast Iron Skillet: I love to cook with a cast iron skillet because it can go straight from stovetop to oven and is an excellent tool for searing and roasting meat. My cast iron skillet was my grandmother's, and every time I use it, I think of her (though I'm sure she wasn't cooking keto!).

Blender: Because we're creating dairy-free recipes, we lose many of the natural binders that help thicken and hold ingredients together. A blender will help quickly incorporate ingredients.

Good Knife: A good sharp knife is essential to make all of your ingredients come together (or apart!) more easily. I personally love Cutco-brand knives.

Baking Sheets: You can cook everything from salmon to cookies on a baking sheet, so it's great to have two or three 13-by-18-inch rimmed baking sheets on hand. Use nonstick pans or layer parchment paper for easy cleanup. Nice to Have Once you've started cooking more often, you might find you'd like a few extra tools to fill out your kitchen arsenal.

Stand Mixer: A stand mixer (rather than a handheld electric mixer) is really nice to have for baking. You can combine your ingredients at the same time as you chop, wash, or perform other kitchen tasks, thereby minimizing your prep time.

Baking Dishes: I use both 9-by-13-inch and 8-by-11-inch baking dishes a lot when I cook keto meals. Baking dishes have deeper sides than rimmed baking sheets, so they work for a wide range of recipes, from roasts to casseroles to desserts. Enameled cast iron baking sheets are pricey but conduct heat extremely well and are also versatile (they can even be used on the stovetop). Tempered glass (like Pyrex) or enameled ceramic baking dishes are the next best thing; they're durable and most are suitable for use with a wide range of oven temperatures.

Mixing Bowls: Having small, medium, and large mixing bowls makes cooking so much simpler. They're easy to store and wash, so you'll always have a clean one handy and appropriately sized for your ingredient (which helps avoid messes in the kitchen due to overfilled bowls).

Splatter Screen: A splatter screen is a game changer for stovetop cooking. You place the screen (usually made of stainless steel or silicone) on top of the active pan to catch any bubbling oils or splashes

Swap It Out!

NEED THIS	USE THIS INSTEAD
Butter for cooking	Olive oil, Avocado oil, Coconut oil
Butter for Spreading	Avocado, Coconut butter
Cream Cheese	Diary-free cream cheese
Greek Yogurt	Diary-free plain yogurt
Heavy Cream	Coconut cream (canned)
Cream for coffee	Diary-free creamers
Milk	Almond milk, cashew milk, coconut milk
Ranch dressing	Avocado oil-or sunflower oil-based dressings (I prefer Primal Kitchen or Tessemae's

Foods You Should Consume More

Meats

- Bison
- Beef
- Beef liver
- Pork
- Chicken
- Seafood
- Sausage (Without fillers)
- Turkey

Low-carb Veggies

- Avocados
- Asparagus
- Broccoli
- Brussels sprouts
- Cabbage
- Cauliflower
- Green beans
- Lettuce
- Kale
- Mushrooms
- Olives
- Okra
- Pickles
- Onions
- Radishes
- Scallions
- Shallots
- Spaghetti squash (in moderation)

Food You Should Consume in Moderation

Nuts & Seeds

- Almonds
- Chia seeds
- Cashews
- Flaxseeds
- Hazelnuts
- Macadamia nuts
- Nut butters
- Peanuts
- Pecans
- Pine nuts
- Pili nuts
- Pistachios
- Walnuts
- Pumpkin seeds

Berries

- Blueberries
- Blackberries
- Strawberries
- Raspberries

Artificial Sweeteners

- Erythritol (E.g. Swerve)
- Monk fruit sweetener
- Stevia

Foods to Avoid

Dairy

- Cream
- Cheese
- Cream Cheese
- Milk
- Yogurt

Carbs

- Breads
- Candy
- Pasta
- Corn
- Rice
- Potatoes
- Winter
- Squashes

Fruits

- Apricots
- Apples
- Bananas
- Dates
- Grapes
- Grapefruit
- Honeydew

Jenny Pale

- Kiwi
- Mangoes
- Oranges
- Peaches
- Prunes

Chapter Two: Breakfast

Hot Chicken and Waffles

Serves: 6

Preparation time: 40 minutes

Ingredients

- 1 recipe Best Fried Chicken Ever
- ¼ cup hot wing sauce
- 1 tablespoon cayenne
- 1 recipe Waffles
- 6 tablespoons sugar-free maple-flavored syrup (such as Choc Zero)
- 2 tablespoons Swerve confectioners

Directions

1. In a bowl, toss the chicken in the hot sauce and cayenne.
2. Arrange the chicken on top of the waffles, drizzle the syrup over the top, sprinkle with powdered sweetener, and serve immediately.

Nutritional Information: Calories: 572, Carbs: 22g, Fat: 48g, Fiber: 4g, Protein: 26g

Sausage Gravy

Serves: 8

Preparation time: 10 minutes

Cooking time: 20 minutes

Ingredients

- 2 tablespoons olive oil
- 1-pound pork sausage
- ½ white onion, diced
- 1 tablespoon minced garlic
- 1 (14-ounce) can coconut milk
- ¼ cup almond flour
- 1 teaspoon amaranth flour
- 1 teaspoon salt
- ½ teaspoon freshly ground pepper

Directions

1. Heat olive oil in a cast iron skillet over medium-high heat. Add sausage and cook, stirring and breaking up the meat with a spatula, until it begins to brown, about 2 minutes
2. Add the onions and garlic, then continue to cook. Stirring frequently, until the sausage is browned and the onion is soft, about 5 minutes.
3. Reduce the heat to medium and clear a space in the center of the meat mixture. Pour the coconut milk into the space. Then, stirring the milk constantly, add the almond and amaranth flours
4. Cook, stirring, until the milk and flours are well combined, about 5 minutes
5. Now stir the milk mixture and the meat together to mix well, and cook for another 3-5 minutes, or until thickened. Don't be alarmed if the texture is thinner than what you might be used to; it will still taste like an old-school, rich, creamy gravy
6. Season with the salt and pepper, and serve hot

Nutritional Information: Calories: 335, Carbs: 4g, Fat: 31g, Fiber: 1g, Protein:

10g

Iced Green Tea Latte

Serves: 8

Preparation time: 3 minutes

Ingredients

- ½ cup hot (not boiling) water
- 1 tablespoon matcha powder
- 8 ounces cold unsweetened cashew milk (or hemp milk if nut-free)
- 5 drops vanilla-flavored liquid stevia

Directions

1. Place the hot water and matcha powder in a blender and pulse until smooth.
2. Add the milk and sweetener and blend well. Pour into a glass over ice.
3. Serve fresh

Nutritional Information: Calories: 38, Carbs: 7g, Fat: 1g, Fiber: 1g, Protein: 1g

Cherry Almond Breakfast Shake

Serves: 2

Preparation time: 4 minutes

Ingredients

- 1 cup unsweetened cashew milk or almond milk (or coconut milk for a thicker drink)
- 1 cup strong brewed cherry or hibiscus tea, chilled (or more cashew milk)
- ¼ cup almond butter
- 1 teaspoon cherry extract
- ½ teaspoon almond extract
- ¼ cup Swerve confectioners
- Pinch of fine sea salt Crushed ice

Directions

1. Place all of the ingredients, except the ice, in a blender and blend until smooth. Just before serving, add the crushed ice and puree again until smooth. Pour into 2 glasses and serve.
2. Store in an airtight container in the refrigerator.

Nutritional Information: Calories: 203, Carbs:7g, Fat: 18g, Fiber: 3g, Protein: 9g

French Toast Cereal

Serves: 1

Preparation time: 15 minutes

Ingredients

- 2 tablespoons melted coconut oil
- 2 tablespoons Swerve confectioners'-style sweetener or equivalent amount of liquid or powdered sweetener
- 1 teaspoon ground cinnamon
- ½ teaspoon maple or vanilla extract
- 1-ounce pork rinds, crumbled into
- ¼- to ½-inch pieces
- 1 cup unsweetened cashew milk

Directions

1. Place the melted coconut oil, sweetener, cinnamon, and extract in a small bowl. Stir well to combine. Add the crumbled pork rinds and stir well to coat.
2. Cover and place the bowl in the refrigerator to chill for at least 10 minutes or until ready to eat (it will keep in an airtight container in the refrigerator for up to 3 days).
3. When ready to eat, uncover and break up the cereal a bit with a spoon. Just before serving, pour in the milk.

Nutritional Information: Calories: 426, Carbs: 4g, Fat: 42g, Fiber: 1g, Protein: 8g

Sausage Breakfast Hash

Serves: 6

Preparation time: 15 minutes

Cooking time: 35 minutes

Ingredients

- 6 tablespoons olive oil
- 1-pound kielbasa, cut into ½-inch pieces
- 1 green bell pepper, seeded and chopped
- 1 red bell pepper, seeded and chopped
- 1 red onion, diced
- 1 jalapeño pepper, diced
- 3 garlic cloves, minced
- 1 teaspoon salt
- ½ teaspoon freshly ground black pepper
- 1 (14-ounce) can stewed tomatoes

Directions

1. In a large skillet, heat the oil over medium heat. Add the kielbasa and cook, stirring, until browned, about 5 minutes.
2. Add the green pepper, red pepper, onion, jalapeño, garlic, salt, and black pepper. Cook, stirring occasionally, for 10 to 12 minutes, until the vegetables are softened and browned.
3. Reduce the heat to medium-low, stir in the tomatoes, cover, and let simmer for 15 minutes. Serve hot.

Nutritional Information: Calories: 331, Carbs: 11g, Fat: 27g, Fiber: 2g, Protein: 11g

Jenny Pale

Truffle Keto Cheesecake

Serves: 1

Preparation time: 2hr 20 minutes

Ingredients

Filling Ingredients

- 40 drops liquid stevia (to taste)
- 10 Tbsp. erythritol, powdered (130 g)
- 1 tsp. vanilla extract
- 7 ounces raw macadamia nuts, soaked overnight, rinsed and drained
- 4 Tbsp. raw cacao butter, melted
- 3 Tbsp. virgin coconut oil, melted
- 2 ounces baking chocolate, melted
- ½ cup cocoa powder (50g)
- ½ cup coconut milk
- ¼ tsp. sea salt

Crust Ingredients

- 2 Tbsp. cocoa powder
- 1 cup blanched almond flour (100 g)
- 3 Tbsp. coconut oil, melted
- Pinch sea salt
- 1 Tbsp. coconut milk

Directions

1. Preheat oven to 350 F. With unbleached parchment paper, line the bottom only of a 7" cheesecake pan

2. Combine the crust ingredients in a small bowl. Mix well to form a dough. The dough should be slightly wet and hold together when pinched. If not, add melted oil by teaspoon.

3. Press dough tightly into the bottom of the lined pan. Poke with a fork to make small holes. Transfer to the oven par-bake for 10-12 minutes. Let cool completely.

4. Make the filling while the crust is cooling.

5. Add the cheesecake filling ingredients in a high-powered blender. Blend on high speed until you achieve a smooth, uniform consistency.

6. Scrape filling into par-baked crust. Tap on the counter to remove air bubbles. Cover loosely with plastic wrap and refrigerate until set - about 8 hours. Alternately, freeze for 2-3 hours, then defrost before cutting.

7. Run a butter knife around the outside edge once set, then unlatch the spring form. If frozen, defrost before cutting.

8. Serve with fresh whipped cream and garnish with chocolate shavings or cinnamon, if you desire.

Nutritional Information: Calories: 245, Carbs: 13g, Fat: 25g, Fiber: 3g, Protein: 4g

Radish Hash Browns with Onion and Green Pepper

Serves: 3

Preparation time: 5 minutes

Cooking time: 25 minutes

Ingredients

- 5 tablespoons olive oil
- 12 radishes, thinly sliced
- 1 onion, diced
- 1 green bell pepper, seeded and diced
- 6 garlic cloves, minced
- 1 teaspoon cayenne
- 1 teaspoon salt
- ½ teaspoon freshly ground black pepper

Directions

1. In a skillet over medium heat, heat the oil. Add the radishes, onion, bell pepper, and garlic. Cook, stirring frequently, until the vegetables are tender, about 5 minutes.
2. Add the cayenne, salt, and pepper. Continue to cook, stirring occasionally, for about 20 minutes, or until the vegetables are browned and crisp around the edges.

Nutritional Information: Calories: 252, Carbs: 8g, Fat: 24g, Fiber: 2g, Protein: 1g

Perfect Bacon

Serves: 4

Preparation time: 5 minutes

Cooking time: 22 minutes

Ingredients

- 1 (12-ounce) package bacon (8 to 12 strips)

Direction

1. Preheat the oven to 400°F.
2. Line a large baking sheet with two pieces of parchment paper.
3. Arrange the bacon strips in a single layer on the prepared sheet.
4. Cook in the preheated oven for 22 minutes.
5. Let cool slightly before serving.

Nutritional Information: Calories: 100, Carbs: 0g, Fat: 8g, Fiber: 0g, Protein: 7g

Keto Faux Cappuccino

Serves: 1

Preparation time: 10 minutes

Ingredients

- ¼ cup nut milk
- 1 scoop vanilla-flavored collagen
- 1 scoop MCT oil powder
- 1 cup brewed coffee

Directions

1. Combine the nut milk, collagen, and MCT oil powder in an electric frothier or a coffee cup. Froth until fluffy and thick. (If using a handheld frothier, heat the mixture for about 20 seconds in the microwave beforehand.)
2. Combine the froth mixture with the coffee and enjoy immediately.

Nutritional Information: Calories: 183, Carbs: 6g, Fat: 11g, Fiber: 0g, Protein: 13g

Cauliflower Oatmeal with Blueberries

Serves: 2

Preparation time: 5 minutes

Cooking Time: 15 minutes

Ingredients

- 1 (12-ounce) bag riced cauliflower
- 1 (14-ounce) can coconut milk
- 2 tablespoons walnut oil
- 2 tablespoons peanut butter powder
- 2 tablespoons sugar-free maple syrup (such as Choc Zero)
- 10 blueberries

Direction

1. In a medium saucepan, combine the cauliflower and coconut milk and bring to a boil over medium-high heat.
2. Reduce the heat to medium-low and stir in the walnut oil, peanut butter powder, and syrup. Cook, stirring occasionally, for 10 minutes.
3. Serve immediately, topped with the blueberries.

Nutritional Information: Calories: 684, Carbs: 27g, Fat: 60g, Fiber: 0g, Protein: 9g

Chapter Three: Staples, Sauces & Dressings

Red Pepper Dry Rub

Serves: ¼ cup

Preparation time: 10 minutes

Ingredients

- 2 teaspoons red pepper flakes
- 2 teaspoons salt
- 1½ teaspoons granulated garlic
- 1½ teaspoons onion powder
- 1½ teaspoons freshly ground black pepper
- 1 teaspoon dry mustard
- 1 teaspoon ground cumin
- ½ teaspoon cloves
- ½ teaspoon dried sage

Directions

1. In a small bowl or jar, combine the red pepper flakes, salt, granulated garlic, onion powder, pepper, dry mustard, cumin, cloves, and sage. Use immediately or store in an airtight container.

Nutritional Information: Calories: 6, Carbs: 1g, Fat: 0g, Fiber: 0g, Protein: 0g

Everything Marinade

Serves: ½ cup

Preparation time: 10 minutes

Ingredients

- 6 tablespoons olive oil
- 3 tablespoons white vinegar
- 1 teaspoon red pepper flakes
- 1 teaspoon whole-grain mustard
- 1 teaspoon salt
- 1 teaspoon freshly ground black pepper
- 1 teaspoon minced garlic

Directions

1. In a small bowl or large zip-top bag, mix the oil, vinegar, red pepper flakes, mustard, salt, pepper, and garlic. Use immediately or store in an airtight container for up to 2 weeks.

Nutritional Information: Calories: 93, Carbs: 1g, Fat: 11g, Fiber: 0g, Protein: 0g

Lemon-Garlic Dressing

Serves: ½ cup

Preparation time: 10 minutes

Ingredients

- Zest and juice of 1 large lemon
- 6 garlic cloves, minced
- 1 teaspoon salt
- 1 teaspoon freshly ground black pepper
- ½ teaspoon Swerve granular (or another granulated alternative sweetener)
- ¾ cup olive oil

Directions

1. In a small bowl, whisk together the lemon zest and juice, garlic, salt, pepper, and sweetener.
2. While whisking, add the olive oil in a thin stream and whisk until the mixture emulsifies. Use immediately or store in an airtight container in the refrigerator for up to 2 weeks.

Nutritional Information: Calories: 223, Carbs: 2g, Fat: 25g, Fiber: 0g, Protein: 0g

Pico De Gallo

Serves: 2 cups

Preparation time: 15 minutes

Ingredients

- 1 large jalapeño pepper, diced
- ½ red onion, diced
- 10 cherry tomatoes, diced
- 8 garlic cloves, minced
- 3 tablespoons avocado oil
- 1½ teaspoons salt
- ½ teaspoon freshly ground black pepper

Directions

1. In a small bowl, combine the jalapeño, onion, tomatoes, and garlic.
2. Add the avocado oil, salt, and black pepper, and mix to combine. Serve immediately or store in an airtight container in the refrigerator for up to 5 days.

Nutritional Information: Calories: 61, Carbs: 3g, Fat: 5g, Fiber: 0g, Protein: 1g

Guacamole

Serves: 2 ½ cups

Preparation time: 20 minutes

Ingredients

- 3 avocados, halved, pitted, and peeled
- ½ red onion, diced
- 1 small tomato, diced
- 1 jalapeño pepper, diced (optional)
- 1 teaspoon garlic salt
- ½ teaspoon freshly ground black pepper

Directions

1. In a small bowl, mash the avocados with a fork until desired consistency is achieved. (I prefer my guacamole chunky.)
2. Add the onion, tomato, and jalapeño (if using), and stir to combine. 3Add the garlic salt and black pepper. Stir and serve immediately.

Nutritional Information: Calories: 200, Carbs: 11g, Fat: 16g, Fiber: 8g, Protein: 3g

Tartar Sauce

Serves: 1 cup

Preparation time: 5 minutes

Ingredients

- 1 cup sugar-free mayonnaise (like Primal Kitchen)
- 3 tablespoons chopped dill pickles
- 1 teaspoon yellow mustard
- 1 teaspoon Swerve granular

Directions

1. In a small bowl or jar, whisk or shake together the mayonnaise, pickles, mustard, and sweetener.
2. Use immediately or store in an airtight container in the refrigerator for up to 1 week.

Nutritional Information: Calories: 211, Carbs: 1g, Fat: 23g, Fiber: 0g, Protein: 0g

Pickled Cucumbers and Onions

Serves: 6

Preparation time: 10 minutes

Ingredients

- 5 or 6 baby cucumbers, diced
- 1 large white onion, diced
- 1 cup white vinegar
- 2 teaspoons chopped fresh dill
- 1½ teaspoons salt
- 1 teaspoon freshly ground black pepper
- 1 teaspoon olive oil

Directions

1. In a mason jar or other airtight container, combine the cucumbers, onion, vinegar, dill, salt, pepper, and olive oil. Serve immediately or cover and store in the refrigerator for up to 2 weeks.

Nutritional Information: Calories: 62, Carbs: 10g, Fat: 2g, Fiber: 2g, Protein: 2g

Herb-Kale Pesto

Serves: 1 ½ cups

Preparation time: 15 minutes

Ingredients

- 1 cup chopped kale
- 1 cup fresh basil leaves
- 3 garlic cloves
- 2 teaspoons nutritional yeast
- ¼ cup extra-virgin olive oil

Directions

2. Place the kale, basil, garlic, and yeast in a food processor and pulse until the mixture is finely chopped, about 3 minutes.
3. With the food processor running, drizzle the olive oil into the pesto until a thick paste forms, scraping down the sides of the bowl at least once.
4. Add a little water if the pesto is too thick.
5. Store the pesto in an airtight container in the refrigerator for up to 1 week.

Nutritional Information: Calories: 44, Carbs: 1g, Fat: 4g, Fiber: 1g, Protein: 1g

Cream Cheese Icing

Serves: 1 ½ cups

Preparation time: 10 minutes

Ingredients

- 1 (8-ounce) container dairy-free cream cheese (such as Kite Hill), at room temperature
- ¼ cup Swerve confectioners' (or another powdered alternative sweetener)
- 1 teaspoon vanilla extract

Directions

1. In a small bowl, blend together the cream cheese, sweetener, and vanilla. Use immediately or refrigerate to stiffen.
2. Store covered in the refrigerator for up to 1 week.

Nutritional Information: Calories: 68, Carbs: 3g, Fat: 4g, Fiber: 0g, Protein: 3g

Chocolate Sauce

Serves: 1 cup

Preparation time: 10 minutes

Cooking time: 15 minutes

Ingredients

- 1 cup cacao butter
- 1 heaping tablespoon raw cacao powder (see tip)
- 2 tablespoons Swerve confectioners' (or another powdered alternative sweetener)

Directions

1. In a small saucepan, melt the cacao butter over medium-low heat.
2. While stirring continuously, add the cacao powder and sweetener. Cook, stirring, until the sweetener is dissolved, about 15 minutes.
3. Serve hot for dipping, store in an airtight container in the refrigerator for up to 2 weeks or freeze for up to 3 months.

Nutritional Information: Calories: 133, Carbs: 0.5g, Fat: 14g, Fiber: 0g, Protein: 1g

Chapter Four: Small Bites, Smoothies and Drinks

Spinach-Blueberry Smoothie

Serves: 1

Preparation time: 5 minutes

Ingredients

- ½ cup blueberries
- 1 scoop plain protein powder
- 2 tablespoons coconut oil
- 4 ice cubes Mint sprigs, for garnish

Directions

1. Put the coconut milk, spinach, cucumber, blueberries, protein powder, coconut oil, and ice in a blender and blend until smooth.
2. Pour into 2 glasses, garnish each with the mint, and serve immediately.

Nutritional Information: Calories: 353, Carbs: 9g, Fat: 32g, Fiber: 3g, Protein: 15g

Low-carb ginger smoothie

Serves: 1 cup

Preparation time: 5 minutes

Ingredients

- 1/6 cup coconut milk or coconut cream
- 1/3 cup water
- 1 tbsp lime juice
- ½ oz. frozen spinach
- 1 tsp fresh ginger, grated

Directions

1. Mix all ingredients together. Start with 1 tablespoon lime and increase the amount to taste.
2. Sprinkle with some grated ginger and serve. So tasty!!

Nutritional Information: Calories: 82, Carbs: 3g, Fat: 8g, Protein: 1g

Virgin Strawberry Margarita

Serves: 4

Preparation time: 4 minutes

Ingredients

- Medium-coarse sea salt
- Lime wedge
- 2 cups strong brewed hibiscus tea, chilled
- ¼ cup Swerve confectioners'-style sweetener
- ¼ cup lime juice
- 2 teaspoons strawberry extract
- Ice, for serving
- 4 lime wedges, for garnish

Directions

1. To coat the rims of the glasses, if desired, fill a saucer with about 1/8 inch of medium-coarse sea salt. Run a lime wedge around the rims of 4 tumblers. Take one of the glasses and roll the edge of the dampened rim in the salt until the entire rim is coated. Repeat with the other 3 glasses.
2. Place the tea, sweetener, lime juice, and extract in a blender and blend until smooth. To serve, carefully fill the salt-rimmed tumblers with ice. Pour the margarita mixture into the glasses and garnish with lime wedges.
3. Store in a pitcher in the refrigerator for up to 5 days. Stir well before serving.

Nutritional Information: Calories: 4, Carbs: 1g, Fat: 0g, Fiber: 0.1g, Protein: 0g

Chocolate Sauce

Serves: 1 cup

Preparation time: 10 minutes

Cooking time: 15 minutes

Ingredients

- 1 cup cacao butter
- 1 heaping tablespoon raw cacao powder (see tip)
- 2 tablespoons Swerve confectioners' (or another powdered alternative sweetener)

Directions

4. In a small saucepan, melt the cacao butter over medium-low heat.
5. While stirring continuously, add the cacao powder and sweetener. Cook, stirring, until the sweetener is dissolved, about 15 minutes.
6. Serve hot for dipping, store in an airtight container in the refrigerator for up to 2 weeks or freeze for up to 3 months.

Nutritional Information: Calories: 133, Carbs: 0.5g, Fat: 14g, Fiber: 0g, Protein: 1g

Creamy Cinnamon Smoothie

Serves: 2

Preparation time: 5 minutes

Ingredients

- 2 cups coconut milk
- 1 scoop vanilla protein powder
- 5 drops liquid stevia
- 1 teaspoon ground cinnamon
- ½ teaspoon alcohol-free vanilla extract

Directions

1. Put the coconut milk, protein powder, stevia, cinnamon, and vanilla in a blender and blend until smooth.
2. Pour into 2 glasses and serve immediately.

Nutritional Information: Calories: 492, Carbs: 8g, Fat: 47g, Fiber: 2g, Protein: 18g

Lemon-Cashew Smoothie

Serves: 1

Preparation time: 5 minutes

Ingredients

- 1 cup unsweetened cashew milk
- ¼ cup heavy (whipping) cream
- ¼ cup freshly squeezed lemon juice
- 1 scoop plain protein powder
- 1 tablespoon coconut oil
- 1 teaspoon sweetener

Directions

1. Put the cashew milk, heavy cream, lemon juice, protein powder, coconut oil, and sweetener in a blender and blend until smooth.
2. Pour into a glass and serve immediately.

Nutritional Information: Calories: 503, Carbs: 15g, Fat: 45g, Protein: 29g

Shrimp Cocktail

Serves: 8

Preparation time: 5 minutes

Ingredients

- ¾ cup tomato sauce
- 1 tablespoon prepared horseradish, or more to taste
- 1 tablespoon lemon juice
- 1 to 2 teaspoons Swerve confectioners'-style sweetener
- ½ teaspoon onion powder
- ½ teaspoon fine sea salt
- 1-pound precooked large shrimp
- 1 lemon, sliced into wedges, for serving (optional)

Directions

1. Make the sauce: Place the sauce ingredients in a small bowl and stir well to combine. Adjust the seasoning to taste.
2. Serve the shrimp with the cocktail sauce, with lemon wedges on the side, if desired. 3.
3. Store in an airtight container in the refrigerator for up to 3 days.

Nutritional Information: Calories: 76, Carbs: 2g, Fat: 1g, Fiber: 14g, Protein: 14g

Pico De Gallo

Serves: 2 ½ cups

Preparation time: 7 minutes

Ingredients

- 1 large tomato, diced (about 1½ cups)
- ½ cup chopped white onions (about 1 medium)
- 2 cloves garlic, minced
- 2 tablespoons lime juice
- 2 tablespoons chopped fresh cilantro
- 1 jalapeño pepper, seeded and finely diced
- ½ teaspoon fine sea salt

Directions

1. Place all of the ingredients in a small bowl and stir until well combined.
2. Store in an airtight container in the refrigerator for up to 5 days.

Nutritional Information: Calories: 32, Carbs: 2g, Fat: 0.1g, Fiber: 1g, Protein: 1g

Citrus Avocado Salsa

Serves: 4

Preparation time: 5 minutes

Ingredients

- 1 cup diced tomatoes
- 1 small avocado, pitted and diced
- ¼ cup chopped fresh cilantro leaves
- 2 tablespoons avocado oil
- 4 drops orange oil, or 1 teaspoon orange extract
- Juice of 1 lime
- Fine sea salt and ground black pepper

Directions

1. Place the tomatoes, avocado, and cilantro in a small bowl. Add the avocado oil, orange oil, and lime juice and stir. Season to taste with salt and pepper.
2. Store in an airtight container in the refrigerator for up to 4 days.

Nutritional Information: Calories: 140, Carbs: 7g, Fat: 13g, Fiber: 3g, Protein: 1g

Herbed Balsamic Dressing

Serves: 1 cup

Preparation time: 4 minutes

Ingredients

- 1 cup extra-virgin olive oil
- ¼ cup balsamic vinegar
- 2 tablespoons chopped fresh oregano
- 1 teaspoon chopped fresh basil
- 1 teaspoon minced garlic Sea salt Freshly ground black pepper

Directions

1. Whisk the olive oil and vinegar in a small bowl until emulsified, about 3 minutes.
2. Whisk in the oregano, basil, and garlic until well combined, about 1 minute.
3. Season the dressing with salt and pepper.
4. Transfer the dressing to an airtight container, and store it in the refrigerator for up to 1 week. Give the dressing a vigorous shake before using it.

Nutritional Information: Calories: 83, Carbs: 0g, Fat: 9g, Fiber: 0g, Protein: 0g

Virgin Strawberry Margarita

Serves: 4

Preparation time: 4 minutes

Ingredients

- Medium-coarse sea salt
- Lime wedge
- 2 cups strong brewed hibiscus tea, chilled
- ¼ cup Swerve confectioners'-style sweetener or equivalent amount of liquid or powdered sweetener
- ¼ cup lime juice
- 2 teaspoons strawberry extract Ice, for serving
- 4 lime wedges, for garnish

Directions

1. To coat the rims of the glasses, if desired, fill a saucer with about 1/8 inch of medium-coarse sea salt. Run a lime wedge around the rims of 4 tumblers. Take one of the glasses and roll the edge of the dampened rim in the salt until the entire rim is coated. Repeat with the other 3 glasses.
2. Place the tea, sweetener, lime juice, and extract in a blender and blend until smooth. To serve, carefully fill the salt-rimmed tumblers with ice. Pour the margarita mixture into the glasses and garnish with lime wedges.
3. Store in a pitcher in the refrigerator for up to 5 days. Stir well before serving.

Nutritional Information: Calories: 4, Carbs: 1g, Fat: 13g, Fiber: 0.1g, Protein: 0g

Spiced-Chocolate Fat Bombs

Serves: 12 fat bombs

Preparation time: 25 minutes

Cooking time: 4 minutes

Ingredients

- ¾ cup coconut oil
- ¼ cup cocoa powder
- ¼ cup almond butter
- ⅛ teaspoon chili powder
- 3 drops liquid stevia

Directions

1. Line a mini muffin tin with paper liners and set aside.
2. Put a small saucepan over low heat and add the coconut oil, cocoa powder, almond butter, chili powder, and stevia.
3. Heat until the coconut oil is melted, then whisk to blend.
4. Spoon the mixture into the muffin cups and place the tin in the refrigerator until the bombs are firm, about 15 minutes.
5. Transfer the cups to an airtight container and store the fat bombs in the freezer until you want to serve them.

Nutritional Information: Calories: 117, Carbs: 2g, Fat: 12g, Fiber: 0g, Protein: 2g

Chapter Five: Sea Foods

Fried Oysters in The Oven

Serves: 4

Preparation time: 20 minutes

Ingredients

- 3 tablespoons olive oil
- 1 teaspoon garlic salt
- 1 teaspoon freshly ground black pepper
- 1 teaspoon red pepper flakes
- 2 cups finely crushed pork rinds
- 24 shucked oysters

Directions

1. Preheat the oven to 400°F.
2. In a small bowl, mix together the olive oil, garlic salt, black pepper, and red pepper flakes.
3. Put the crushed pork rinds in a separate bowl.
4. Dip each oyster first in the oil mixture to coat and then in the pork rinds, turning to coat. Arrange the coated oysters on a baking sheet in a single layer with room in between.
5. Bake in the preheated oven for 30 minutes, or until the pork rind "breading" is browned and crisp. Serve hot.

Nutritional Information: Calories: 230, Carbs: 5g, Fat: 17g, Fiber: 0g, Protein: 15g

Tuna with Greens and Blueberries

Serves: 2

Preparation time: 10 minutes

Cooking time: 5 minutes

Ingredients

- ¼ cup olive
- 2 (4-ounce) tuna steaks
- Salt
- Freshly ground black pepper
- Juice of 1 lemon
- 4 cups salad greens
- ¼ cup low-carb, diary-free ranch dressing (Tessemae's)
- 2o blueberries

Directions

1. In a large skillet, heat the olive oil over medium-high heat.
2. Season the tuna steaks generously with salt and pepper, and add them to the skillet. Cook for 2 or 2 ½ minutes in each side to sear the outer edges.
3. Squeeze the lemon over the tuna in the pan and remove the fish
4. To serve, arrange the greens on 2 serving plates. Top each plate with one of the tuna steaks, 2 tablespoons of the ranch dressing, and 10 of the blueberries.

Nutritional Information: Calories: 549, Carbs: 7g, Fat: 41g, Fiber: 3g, Protein: 38g

Coconut Shrimp

Serves: 4

Preparation time: 20 minutes

Cooking time: 30 minutes

Ingredients

- Avocado oil spray (or other cooking oil spray)
- 3 large egg whites
- 1 teaspoon cayenne
- 1 teaspoon garlic salt
- 1 teaspoon freshly ground black pepper
- ½ teaspoon Swerve granular (or another granulated alternative sweetener)
- 1 cup unsweetened shredded coconut
- 24 (or so) raw shrimp, peeled

Directions

1. Preheat the oven to 350°F. Spray a large baking sheet with the avocado oil spray.
2. In a small bowl, whisk together the egg whites, cayenne, garlic salt, pepper, and sweetener.
3. Put the shredded coconut in a separate bowl.
4. One at a time, dunk the shrimp first in the egg mixture and then in the coconut, turning to coat completely.
5. Arrange the coated shrimp on the prepared baking sheet in a single layer, with room in between. Once all the shrimp have been coated, spray them lightly with avocado oil spray.
6. Bake in the preheated oven for 30 minutes, or until the coconut is golden brown.

Nutritional Information: Calories: 223, Carbs: 7g, Fat: 17g, Fiber: 4g, Protein: 13g

Bacon-Wrapped Scallop Cups

Serves: 4

Preparation time: 10 minutes

Cooking time: 25 minutes

Ingredients

- 12 large sea scallops
- 6 strips bacon, halved to make 12 short strips
- 24 garlic cloves, peeled but left whole
- 5 tablespoons Lemon-Garlic Dressing

Directions

1. Preheat the oven to 400°F.
2. Wrap each scallop with 1 piece of bacon. Use a toothpick to secure the bacon to the scallop. Arrange the wrapped scallops on a baking sheet.
3. Place 2 garlic cloves on top of each scallop, then top with a spoonful of the dressing. 4Bake for 25 minutes, or until the bacon is browned and crisp.

Nutritional Information: Calories: 374, Carbs: 9g, Fat: 26g, Fiber: 4g, Protein: 26g

Salmon Patties

Serves: 5

Preparation time: 10 minutes

Cooking time: 15 minutes

Ingredients

- 2 (6-ounce) cans boneless salmon
- 1 large egg
- 1½ tablespoons chopped fresh dill
- 1 teaspoon salt
- 1 teaspoon freshly ground black pepper
- 3 tablespoons olive oil

Directions

1. Mix together the salmon, egg, dill, salt and pepper in a small mixing bowl. Form the salmon mixture into hamburger-size patties
2. In a skillet over medium heat, heat the olive oil. Add the salmon patties to the skillet and cook for 3 to 4 minutes per side, or until golden brown and crisp. Serve hot

Nutritional Information: Calories: 198, Carbs: 1g, Fat: 14g, Fiber: 0g, Protein: 17g

Country Club Crab Cakes

Serves: 4

Preparation time: 10 minutes

Cooking time: 20 minutes

Ingredients

- 2 (6-ounce) cans crabmeat (or 12 ounces cooked crabmeat)
- 2 large eggs
- 2 tablespoons chopped fresh dill
- 1 teaspoon garlic salt
- ¼ cup olive oil

Directions

1. In a medium bowl, combine the crabmeat, eggs, dill, and garlic salt. Form the mixture into four patties.
2. In a medium skillet, heat the olive oil over medium heat. Cook the crab cakes for 3 to 4 minutes on each side, or until golden brown.

Nutritional Information: Calories: 212, Carbs: 1g, Fat: 16g, Fiber: 0g, Protein: 16g

Shrimp Sti-fry

Serves: 4

Preparation time: 10 minutes

Cooking time: 20 minutes

Ingredients

- ¼ cup avocado oil
- ¼ cup coconut aminos
- 2 cups chopped broccoli
- 1 onion, diced
- 1 red bell pepper, chopped
- 24 cooked and peeled shrimp
- 1 (12-ounce) bag riced cauliflower
- Chili sauce, for serving (Optional)

Directions

1. Combine the shrimp, Cauliflower, onion, pepper, broccoli, coconut aminos, and avocado oil in a large skillet. Cook, stirring occasionally, until all the flavors are combined, about 20 minutes
2. Drizzle the chili sauce over the top and serve hot

Nutritional Information: Calories: 231, Carbs: 12g, Fat: 15g, Fiber: 5g, Protein: 12g

Baked Salmon with Lemon and Mush

Serves: 2

Preparation time: 10 minutes

Cooking time: 30 minutes

Ingredients

- 2 (6-ounce) skin-on salmon fillets
- 1 onion, diced
- 8 ounces mushrooms, sliced
- ¼ cup olive oil
- 1 teaspoon salt
- 1 teaspoon freshly ground black pepper
- 4 lemon slices

Directions

1. Preheat the oven to 400°F.
2. Tear off 2 large squares of aluminum foil. Place a salmon fillet on each piece of foil and arrange the onion and mushrooms over and around the fish, dividing evenly.
3. Pour the olive oil over the fish, then season with the salt and pepper. Top each piece of fish with 2 lemon slices.
4. Wrap the foil up around the salmon and vegetables, leaving room inside the packet for heat to circulate, and bake for 30 minutes, or until the fish flakes easily with a fork. Serve hot.

Nutritional Information: Calories: 576, Carbs: 8g, Fat: 44g, Fiber: 3g, Protein: 37g

Jenny Pale

Pan-fried Soft Shell Crab

Serves: 2

Preparation time: 5 minutes

Cooking time: 10 minutes

Ingredients

- ½ cup olive oil
- ½ cup almond flour
- 1 teaspoon paprika
- 1 teaspoon garlic salt
- 1 teaspoon freshly ground black pepper
- 2 soft-shell crabs

Directions

1. Fill the bottom of a heavy skillet with the oil and heat over low heat.
2. While the oil is heating, in a medium bowl, mix together the almond flour, paprika, garlic salt, and pepper.
3. Dredge each crab in the flour mixture, coating both sides and shaking off any excess. Put the crabs into the hot oil in the skillet and cook for about 5 minutes per side, or until golden brown.
4. Serve hot.

Nutritional Information: Calories: 489, Carbs: 6g, Fat: 33g, Fiber: 2g, Protein: 42g

Mussels with Lemon-Garlic Sauce and Parsley

Serves: 5

Preparation time: 10 minutes

Cooking time: 5 minutes

Ingredients

- 36 live mussels, scrubbed and debearded
- 1 tablespoon olive oil
- 6 tablespoons Lemon-Garlic Dressing
- 2 tablespoons chopped fresh parsley, for garnish

Directions

1. Fill a stockpot halfway with water and bring it to a boil.
2. Add the mussels and olive oil to the boiling water and continue to boil for 4 minutes. Carefully drain off the water.
3. Pour the dressing over the mussels and serve immediately, garnished with the parsley.

Nutritional Information: Calories: 230, Carbs: 3g, Fat: 18g, Fiber: 1g, Protein: 14g

Three-Minute Lobster Tail

Serves: 2

Preparation time: 5 minutes

Cooking time: 5 minutes

Ingredients

- 4 cups bone broth (or water)
- 2 lobster tails

Directions

1. In a large pot, bring the broth to a boil.
2. While the broth is coming to a boil, use kitchen shears to cut the back side of the lobster shell from end to end.
3. Place the lobster in the boiling broth and bring it back to a boil. Cook the lobster for 3 minutes.
4. Drain and serve immediately.

Nutritional Information: Calories: 154, Carbs: 0g, Fat: 2g, Fiber: 0g, Protein: 32g

Chapter Six: Soups and Salads

Cauliflower and Bacon Soup

Serves: 8

Preparation time: 10 minutes

Cooking time: 1 hour

Ingredients

- 1 head cauliflower, stemmed and cut into large pieces
- 2 (14-ounce) cans coconut milk
- 2 cups bone broth
- 6 tablespoons olive oil, divided
- 1 onion, diced
- 1 cup sliced mushrooms
- 6 garlic cloves, minced
- 1½ teaspoons salt
- 1½ teaspoons freshly ground black pepper
- 1½ teaspoons cayenne
- 1 batch Perfect Bacon, chopped or crumbled

Directions

1. Fill a stockpot halfway with water and add the cauliflower. Bring to a boil and cook until the cauliflower is tender, about 20 minutes. Drain the cauliflower and then return it to the stockpot. Using a potato masher, mash the cauliflower until mostly smooth.
2. Put the pot over low heat and add the coconut milk and broth.
3. In a separate skillet, heat 3 tablespoons of oil over medium heat. Add the onion, mushrooms, and garlic. Cook, stirring frequently, for 15 to 20 minutes, or until softened.

4. Add the onion mixture to the soup mixture and continue cooking over low heat for 5 to 7 more minutes.

5. Stir in the salt, pepper, cayenne, the remaining 3 tablespoons of oil, and the bacon. Cook for 20 minutes more.

6. Serve immediately or store the soup in an airtight container in the refrigerator for up to 1 week.

Nutritional Information: Calories: 414, Carbs: 8g, Fat: 34g, Fiber: 4g, Protein: 19g

Hearty Vegetable Soup

Serves: 8

Preparation time: 30 minutes

Cooking time: 8 hours

Ingredients

- 8 cups vegetable broth
- 2 (14-ounce) cans diced tomatoes
- 1 (16-ounce) bag kale, chopped
- 1 bunch radishes (about 12), halved
- 1 onion, chopped
- 2 celery stalks, chopped
- 2 cups fresh or frozen green beans, cut into 2-inch pieces
- 1 cup whole mushrooms
- 4 garlic cloves, minced
- ¼ cup olive oil

Directions

1. In a slow cooker, combine the vegetable broth, tomatoes, kale, radishes, onion, celery, green beans, mushrooms, garlic, and olive oil
2. Cover and cook on low for 8 hours. Serve hot

Nutritional Information: Calories: 168, Carbs: 15g, Fat: 8g, Fiber: 4g, Protein: 9g

Pizza Soup

Serves: 4

Preparation time: 6 minutes

Cooking time: 30 minutes

Ingredients

- 1 tablespoon avocado oil, coconut oil, or lard
- 2 cups sliced mushrooms
- ¼ cup diced onions
- ¼ cup diced red bell peppers
- 2 cloves garlic, minced
- 4 ounces Italian sausage, cut into ¼-inch pieces
- 4 ounces uncured pepperoni, cut into quarters
- 1 (25-ounce) jar pizza sauce or marinara sauce
- 1 (14½-ounce) can fire-roasted tomatoes
- 1 (3-ounce) can sliced black olives
- 1 tablespoon dried ground oregano
- ½ teaspoon fine sea salt
- Fresh oregano or basil leaves, for garnish

Directions

1. Heat the oil in a deep cast-iron skillet or pot over medium heat. Add the mushrooms and onions and sauté until the mushrooms are golden brown and the onions are soft, about 5 minutes. Add the bell peppers and garlic and sauté for another 2 minutes.
2. Add the sausage and sauté until cooked through, about 3 minutes. Add the pepperoni, pizza sauce, tomatoes, olives (if using), oregano, and salt. Cook for another 15 minutes. Taste and adjust the seasoning to your liking.

3. Ladle the soup into bowls. Garnish with oregano or basil leaves and serve.
4. Store in an airtight container in the refrigerator for up to 3 days. To reheat, place the soup in a saucepan over medium heat for a few minutes, until warmed through.

Nutritional Information: Calories: 430, Carbs: 17g, Fat: 35g, Fiber: 5g, Protein: 15g

Stuffed-Pepper Soup

Serves: 8

Preparation time: 20 minutes

Cooking time: 1 hours

Ingredients

- 4 tablespoons olive oil, divided
- 1-pound ground beef
- 4 cups bone broth
- 1 (12-ounce) can tomato sauce
- 1 (12-ounce) bag riced cauliflower
- 1 (3.8-ounce) can diced black olives, drained
- 2 green bell peppers, diced
- 3 tablespoons minced garlic

Directions

1. In a large pot, heat 2 tablespoons of oil over medium-high heat. Add the beef and cook, stirring, until browned, about 5 minutes.
2. Add the broth, tomato sauce, cauliflower, olives, peppers, and garlic, and bring to a simmer.
3. Reduce the heat to low and let simmer for about 1 hour, or until the soup is thickened and the flavors have melded. Serve hot.

Nutritional Information: Calories: 286, Carbs: 8g, Fat: 18g, Fiber: 3g, Protein: 23g

Broccoli Salad

Serves: 6

Preparation time: 10 minutes

Ingredients

- 1 (12-ounce) bag broccoli slaw (or 1 head broccoli, chopped or shredded)
- 1½ cups low-carb mayonnaise (like Primal Kitchen)
- 6 tablespoons salted sunflower seeds
- ½ cup chopped red onion
- ¼ cup white vinegar
- 4 strips Perfect Bacon, chopped
- 2 teaspoons Swerve granular (or another granulated alternative sweetener)
- 5 red grapes (optional)

Directions

1. In an airtight container, mix the broccoli slaw, mayonnaise, sunflower seeds, onion, vinegar, bacon, sweetener, and grapes (if using).
2. Cover and chill for at least 2 hours. Serve cold. Store in an airtight container in the refrigerator for up to 3 days.

Nutritional Information: Calories: 564, Carbs: 7g, Fat: 56g, Fiber: 2g, Protein: 7g

Chilled Tomato and Ham Soup

Serves: 6

Preparation time: 5 minutes plus 15 minutes to chill

Ingredients

- ¾ pound plum tomatoes, quartered
- 1 clove garlic, whacked with the side of a large knife and peeled
- ¼ cup avocado oil
- 1 tablespoon coconut vinegar, plus more for serving
- Fine sea salt and ground black pepper
- 4 thin slices prosciutto (about 1 ounce), sliced into strips about ¼ inch wide
- Fresh herbs of choice, for garnish (optional)

Directions

1. Place the tomatoes, garlic, oil, and vinegar in a blender or food processor and pulse until smooth. Season with salt and pepper and refrigerate for about 15 minutes, until cold.
2. Press the eggs through a sieve or colander with tiny holes.
3. Ladle the chilled soup into bowls and drizzle a little vinegar and oil on top. Serve the soup topped with the sieved hard-boiled eggs and strips of ham. Garnish with fresh herbs, if desired.
4. Store in an airtight container in the refrigerator for up to 3 days. To reheat, place the soup in a saucepan over medium heat for a few minutes, until warmed through.

Nutritional Information: Calories: 406, Carbs: 8g, Fat: 36g, Fiber: 2g, Protein: 15g

Chinese Beef and Broccoli Soup

Serves: 8

Preparation time: 10 minutes

Cooking time: 18 minutes

Ingredients

- 2 pounds cubed beef stew meat
- 1 tablespoon wheat-free tamari, or
- ¼ cup coconut aminos
- 2 tablespoons plus
- 2 teaspoons coconut oil, divided
- 1 cup diced onions
- 5 cloves garlic, minced
- 1 tablespoon peeled and grated fresh ginger (optional)
- ¼ teaspoon fine sea salt
- ½ teaspoon ground black pepper
- 6 cups broccoli florets, cut into bite-sized pieces
- 6 cups beef bone broth
- 2 tablespoons fish sauce
- 2 tablespoons Swerve confectioners
- Scallions, sliced diagonally, for garnish

Directions

1. If any of the stew meat pieces are larger than about 1 inch, cut them down to size. Place the meat in a medium-sized bowl.
2. Add the tamari and toss to coat. Place in the refrigerator to marinate for at least 1 hour or overnight.

3. Heat 1 tablespoon of coconut oil in a large pot or Dutch oven over medium-high heat. When the oil is rippling hot, add half of the beef. Spread the beef across the pot and cook, without stirring, for 1 minute. Stir or toss with tongs, spread the beef across the pot again, and cook for 1 minute more. Be careful not to overcook the meat; it should be just barely cooked through and still very tender. Transfer the meat to a dish with a lid.

4. Drain any excess liquid from the pot. Repeat Step 2 with another tablespoon of coconut oil and the remaining meat.

5. Add the second batch of cooked meat and any juices from the pot to the dish and cover tightly with the lid.

6. Add the remaining 2 teaspoons of coconut oil and the onions, garlic, and ginger, if using, to the hot pot. Toss to coat the onions with the oil, sprinkle with the salt and pepper, and cook for about 5 minutes, stirring occasionally, until the onions are tender.

7. Add the broccoli and beef broth and bring to a simmer. Stir in the fish sauce and sweetener and taste; add more salt or sweetener, if desired. Simmer for 4 minutes or until the broccoli is soft.

8. Remove from the heat and stir in the cooked meat and any juices. Ladle the soup into bowls, garnish with sliced scallions, and serve.

9. Store in an airtight container in the refrigerator for up to 3 days. To reheat, place the soup in a saucepan over medium heat for a few minutes, until warmed through.

Nutritional Information: Calories: 426, Carbs: 7g, Fat: 28g, Fiber: 4g, Protein: 35g

Turkey and Orzo Soup

Serves: 8

Preparation time: 10 minutes

Cooking time: 18 minutes

Ingredients

- 1 tablespoon coconut oil
- 2 tablespoons finely diced onions
- 2 cups coarsely chopped cauliflower florets
- 6 cups chicken bone broth, homemade or store-bought
- 1½ cups diced roasted turkey or chicken
- Fine sea salt (optional)
- 3 tablespoons chopped fresh dill, plus extra for garnish
- Freshly ground black pepper, for garnish

Directions

1. Melt the coconut oil in a Dutch oven or stockpot over medium-high heat. Add the onions and sauté for 4 minutes or until translucent. Add the cauliflower and sauté for another 3 minutes. Add the broth, turkey, and dill and simmer for 3 minutes or until heated through. Taste and add salt, if needed.
2. Ladle the soup into bowls and garnish with a sprig of dill and some freshly ground pepper before serving.
3. Store in an airtight container in the refrigerator for up to 3 days. To reheat, place the soup in a saucepan over medium heat for a few minutes, until warmed through.

Nutritional Information: Calories: 179, Carbs: 17g, Fat: 18g, Fiber: 2g, Protein: `8g

Coconut Ginger Chicken Soup

Serves: 8

Preparation time: 10 minutes

Cooking time: 50 minutes

Ingredients

- ¼ cup peeled and grated fresh ginger
- 3 cloves garlic, chopped
- 4 stalks lemongrass, hard outer layers removed and top third discarded, then chopped
- 3 shallots, chopped
- 1 teaspoon ground white pepper
- 4 cups full-fat coconut milk
- 4 boneless, skinless chicken breast halves (about 2 pounds), chopped into bite-sized pieces
- Grated zest of 2 limes
- 3 tablespoons fish sauce
- 5 serrano chile peppers, minced (seeded for less heat)
- ½ teaspoon fine sea salt

Directions

1. Make the ginger paste: Place the ginger and garlic in a food processor or mortar and pulse or pound (using the pestle) into a paste. Add the lemongrass, shallots, and white pepper and pulverize. Set aside.

2. In a medium-sized saucepan, bring the coconut milk to a gentle simmer over medium heat. Do not overheat or it will curdle. Add the ginger paste and stir well, then add the chicken and bring to a boil. Add the lime zest, fish sauce, chiles, and salt. Cover and simmer over medium-low heat for about 45 minutes, until the chicken is fully cooked.

3. Ladle the soup into bowls, then garnish with chives, cilantro, and lime wedges and serve.

4. Store in an airtight container in the refrigerator for up to 3 days. To reheat, place the soup in a saucepan over medium heat for a few minutes, until warmed through.

Nutritional Information: Calories: 441, Carbs: 7g, Fat: 27g, Fiber: 1g, Protein: 39g

Manhattan Clam Chowder

Serves: 4

Preparation time: 8 minutes

Cooking time: 20 minutes

Ingredients

- 4 strips bacon, diced
- ¼ cup diced onions
- 2 cloves garlic, minced
- 1 stalk celery, diced
- 1 green bell pepper, diced
- 1 small zucchini, diced
- ½ teaspoon dried thyme leaves
- 1 teaspoon fine sea salt
- ½ teaspoon ground black pepper
- 1 large tomato, diced, with juices
- 2 tablespoons tomato paste
- 4 cups chicken bone broth, homemade or store-bought
- 1 (8-ounce) bottle clam juice
- 2 bay leaves
- 2 (10-ounce) cans baby clams with liquid

For Garnish

- Avocado oil or extra-virgin olive oil
- Chopped fresh parsley, oregano, or other herb of choice

Directions

1. Sauté the bacon in a stockpot or Dutch oven over medium-high heat until crisp, about 4 minutes.

2. Add the onions and garlic to the pot and sauté for 2 minutes, then add the celery, bell pepper, zucchini, and thyme. Season the veggies with the salt and pepper and sauté for 4 more minutes.

3. Add the tomato, tomato paste, broth, clam juice, and bay leaves. Bring to a boil, then lower the heat and simmer for 10 minutes.

4. Just before serving, add the clams and cook just until the clams are warmed through. Taste and add more seasoning, if desired. Ladle the soup into bowls and garnish with a drizzle of oil and parsley leaves.

5. Store in an airtight container in the refrigerator for up to 3 days. To reheat, place the soup in a saucepan over medium heat for a few minutes, until warmed through.

Nutritional Information: Calories: 306, Carbs: 13g, Fat: 14g, Fiber: 3g, Protein: 14g

Wedge Salad with Ranch Dressing
Serves: 4

Preparation time: 20 minutes

Ingredients

- 1 head iceberg lettuce, cut into 4 wedges
- ½ cup low-carb, dairy-free ranch dressing (such as Tessemae's)
- 6 tablespoons bacon bits
- 1 tomato, diced
- 4 radishes, diced
- ¼ cup chopped fresh chives
- ½ teaspoon freshly ground black pepper

Directions

1. Arrange the lettuce wedges on 4 serving plates. Top each wedge with 2 tablespoons of dressing. Add the bacon bits, tomato, radishes, chives, and pepper. Serve immediately.

Nutritional Information: Calories: 201, Carbs: 6g, Fat: 17g, Fiber: 1g, Protein: 6g

Cold Cauliflower "Pasta" Salad

Serves: 8

Preparation time: 15 minutes

Ingredients

- 2 (12-ounce) bags riced cauliflower
- 1 red bell pepper, seeded and diced
- 1 cup diced dried salami
- 1 cucumber, diced
- ¼ cup olive oil
- 2 tablespoons minced garlic
- 1 teaspoon salt

Directions

1. In the microwave, cook the cauliflower rice according to the package directions. Refrigerate for at least 30 minutes.
2. Add the bell pepper, salami, cucumber, olive oil, garlic, and salt. Mix well, then cover and refrigerate for at least 2 hours to chill.
3. Serve cold or store in an airtight container in the refrigerator for up to 1 week.

Nutritional Information: Calories: 208, Carbs: 7g, Fat: 16g, Fiber: 3g, Protein: 9g

Smoky Spicy Chicken Stew

Serves: 12

Preparation time: 7 minutes

Cooking time: 16 minutes

Ingredients

- 1 tablespoon lard or coconut oil
- 2 pounds ground chicken
- 2 boneless, skinless chicken thighs, cut into ½-inch dice
- 1 cup chopped onions
- 3 tablespoons minced garlic
- 2 tablespoons smoked paprika
- 1 tablespoon ground cumin
- 1 tablespoon dried oregano leaves
- 2 teaspoons fine sea salt
- 1 teaspoon cayenne pepper
- 1 (28-ounce) can diced tomatoes, with juices
- 2 cups chicken bone broth, homemade or store-bought
- 1 (12-ounce) can lime-flavored sparkling water or seltzer water
- 1-ounce unsweetened baking chocolate, finely chopped
- ¼ cup lime juice
- ¼ cup chopped fresh cilantro

For Garnish

- Chopped fresh cilantro
- Lime wedges or slices

- Crushed red pepper

Directions

1. Combine the lard, ground chicken, diced chicken thighs, and onions in a large soup pot over medium-high heat. Cook until the onions are soft and the chicken is cooked through, about 6 minutes.

2. Add the garlic, paprika, cumin, oregano, salt, and cayenne to the pot and sauté for another minute, while stirring. Add the tomatoes with juices, broth, sparkling water, and chocolate. Simmer gently for 10 minutes to allow the flavors to develop.

3. Just before serving, stir in the lime juice and cilantro. Garnish with additional cilantro, lime wedges or slices, and some crushed red pepper, if desired.

4. Store in an airtight container in the refrigerator for up to 3 days. To reheat, place the stew in a saucepan over medium heat for 5 minutes or until warmed through.

Nutritional Information: Calories: 278, Carbs: 6g, Fat: 16g, Fiber: 2g, Protein: 26g

Simple Ham Salad

Serves: 4

Preparation time: 10 minutes

Ingredients

- 2 cups diced ham
- ¾ cup low-carb mayonnaise (such as Primal Kitchen)
- 2 celery stalks, diced

Directions

1. In a small bowl, combine the ham, mayonnaise, and celery, and stir to mix well. Serve immediately or store, covered, in the refrigerator for up to 1 week.

Nutritional Information: Calories: 434, Carbs: 3g, Fat: 42g, Fiber: 1g, Protein: 11g

Thai Red Curry Shrimp Soup

Serves: 4

Preparation time: 5 minutes

Cooking time: 25-45 minutes

Ingredients

- 1 tablespoon avocado oil or coconut oil
- 1-pound medium shrimp, peeled and deveined
- Fine sea salt and ground black pepper
- 3 shallots, finely diced
- 1½ cups chicken bone broth, homemade or store-bought
- 1 (13½-ounce) can full-fat coconut milk
- 1½ tablespoons red curry paste
- ¼ cup fresh cilantro leaves
- ¼ cup scallion pieces (about ½ inch long)
- Juice of 1 lime

For Garnish

- Sliced scallions
- Fresh cilantro leaves Lime wedges

Directions

1. Heat the oil in a large cast-iron skillet over medium heat. Season the shrimp with salt and pepper and sauté for 2 minutes or until cooked through. Remove from the pan and set aside.

2. Add the shallots and sauté until tender, about 2 minutes. Reduce the heat to low. Whisk in the broth, coconut milk, and curry paste. Simmer, uncovered, stirring often, for 10 minutes or until the broth has reduced a bit. The longer you simmer, the thicker your sauce will be.

3. Stir in the cilantro, scallions, and lime juice. Return the shrimp to the pan and stir to coat in the sauce. Immediately remove the pan from the heat

and ladle the soup into bowls. Garnish with sliced scallions, cilantro leaves, and lime wedges.

4. Store in an airtight container in the refrigerator for up to 4 days. To reheat, place the soup in a saucepan over medium heat for 4 minutes or until warmed through.

Nutritional Information: Calories: 362, Carbs: 6g, Fat: 23g, Fiber: 1g, Protein: 32g

Chicken Salad with Grapes and Almonds

Serves: 8

Preparation time: 20 minutes

Ingredients

- 6 boneless, skinless chicken breasts
- 3 tablespoons olive oil
- 1½ cups sugar-free mayonnaise (such as Primal Kitchen)
- ½ cup diced celery
- 10 grapes, diced (optional)
- ¼ cup slivered almonds
- 3 tablespoons poppy seeds
- 1 tablespoon chopped fresh dill
- 1 tablespoon dry mustard

Directions

1. Place the chicken breasts in a stockpot and cover completely with water. Bring to a boil and cook until the chicken is cooked through, about 20 minutes. Drain.
2. Put the chicken in a blender or food processor with the olive oil. Pulse until the chicken is very finely chopped.
3. In a large bowl, combine the chicken with the mayonnaise, celery, grapes (if using), almonds, poppy seeds, dill, and mustard. Serve immediately or cover and refrigerate for up to 1 week.

Nutritional Information: Calories: 506, Carbs: 2g, Fat: 46g, Fiber: 1g, Protein: 21g

Ham and Fauxtato Soup

Serves: 8

Preparation time: 5 minutes

Cooking time: 15 minutes

Ingredients

- 3½ cups chopped cauliflower florets
- ⅓ cup diced celery
- ⅓ cup finely chopped onions
- ¾ cup diced cooked ham
- 3¼ cups chicken bone broth, homemade or store-bought
- ½ teaspoon sea salt
- 1 teaspoon ground black pepper
- 5 tablespoons Kite Hill brand cream cheese style spread

Directions

1. Combine the cauliflower, celery, onions, ham, broth, salt, and pepper in a stockpot. Bring to a boil, then cover and cook over medium heat until the cauliflower is tender, 10 to 15 minutes.
2. Remove from the heat and scoop about half of the hot soup into a blender or food processor. Add the cream cheese spread and pulse until very smooth. Return the puree to the pot and stir to combine. Taste and add more salt and pepper, if desired. Ladle the soup into bowls and serve immediately.
3. Store in an airtight container in the refrigerator for up to 4 days or freeze in a freezer-safe container for up to a month. To reheat, place the soup in a saucepan over medium heat for 4 minutes or until warmed through.

Nutritional Information: Calories: 118, Carbs: 4g, Fat: 8g, Fiber: 1g, Protein: 7g

Salmon Soup

Serves: 8

Preparation time: 10 minutes

Cooking time: 20 minutes

Ingredients

- 1 tablespoon avocado oil or coconut oil
- ¼ cup thinly sliced red onions
- 2 tablespoons minced garlic
- 1-pound skinned salmon fillets, cut into 1-inch chunks
- 1 large tomato, seeded and coarsely chopped
- 1 tablespoon fish sauce
- ¼ teaspoon fine sea salt
- 4 cups fish or chicken bone broth, homemade or store-bought
- 3 tablespoons chopped fresh dill

For Garnish:

- Sprigs of fresh dill Capers
- Sliced fresh chives (optional)
- Freshly ground black pepper

Directions

1. Heat the oil in a saucepan over medium heat. Add the onions and cook for 4 minutes or until soft, stirring occasionally. Add the garlic and sauté for another minute or until fragrant.

2. Add the salmon, tomato, fish sauce (if using), salt, and broth. Bring to a boil over high heat, then reduce the heat to low and simmer gently for 12 minutes or until the salmon is cooked through. Serve immediately, garnished with sprigs of fresh dill, capers, chives (if using), and freshly ground pepper.

3. Store in an airtight container in the refrigerator for up to 3 days. To reheat, place in a saucepan over medium heat for 5 minutes or until warmed through.

Nutritional Information: Calories: 259, Carbs: 4g, Fat: 14g, Fiber: 1g, Protein: 27g

Spicy Shrimp Salad

Serves: 8

Preparation time: 10 minutes

Ingredients

- 3 dozen shrimp, cooked and peeled
- ¼ cup avocado oil
- 1 tablespoon chopped fresh cilantro
- 1 teaspoon cayenne
- 1 teaspoon garlic salt
- 1 teaspoon freshly ground black pepper

Directions

1. In a large bowl, mix together the shrimp, avocado oil, cilantro, cayenne, garlic salt, and pepper.
2. Serve immediately or store in an airtight container in the refrigerator for up to 5 days.

Nutritional Information: Calories: 561, Carbs: 5g, Fat: 44g, Fiber: 1g, Protein: 37g

Chapter Seven: Poultry Recipes

Slow-Cooker Buffalo Chicken

Serves: 8

Preparation time: 10 minutes

Cooking time: 4 hours

Ingredients

- 6 boneless, skinless chicken breasts
- 1 cup hot wing sauce (such as Frank's Red-hot)
- 1 (8-ounce) container dairy-free cream cheese (such as Kite Hill)
- 1 onion, diced (optional)
- ¼ cup olive oil

Directions

1. In the slow cooker, combine the chicken, hot sauce, cream cheese, onion (if using), and olive oil. Cover and cook on low for 7 hours or on high for 4 hours.
2. Once cooked, transfer the chicken breasts to a cutting board and use two forks to shred the meat. Return the meat to the sauce in the pot.
3. Serve hot, as a dip, with a side, or straight from the bowl.

Nutritional Information: Calories: 218, Carbs: 1g, Fat: 14g, Fiber: 0g, Protein: 22g

Salt-And-Pepper Chicken Kebabs with Pineapple

Serves: 6

Preparation time: 15 minutes

Cooking time: 30 minutes

Ingredients

- 6 boneless, skinless chicken breasts, cut into
- 2-inch pieces
- ¼ cup olive oil, plus
- 2 tablespoons more for greasing the skewers
- 2 teaspoons salt
- 1 teaspoon freshly ground black pepper
- 12 (2-inch) chunks pineapple
- 1 green bell pepper, seeded and cut into squares
- 1 onion, cut into 2-inch pieces
- 8 ounces whole mushrooms

Directions

1. Preheat the oven to 400°F.
2. In a large bowl, toss the chicken pieces with the olive oil, salt, and pepper.
3. Grease 6 metal skewers with olive oil (so the chicken will be easier to remove when you eat it later). Thread the pineapple, chicken, pepper, onion, and mushrooms onto the skewers, starting and ending each skewer with pineapple.
4. Lay the skewers on a large rimmed baking sheet and cover with the remaining 2 tablespoons oil. Bake for 30 minutes, or until browned and cooked through.

Nutritional Information: Calories: 293, Carbs: 7g, Fat: 17g, Fiber: 3g, Protein: 28g

Umami Chicken Burgers

Serves: 4

Preparation time: 10 minutes

Cooking time: 20 minutes

Ingredients

- 5 tablespoons olive oil, divided
- 12 ounces spinach
- 1-pound ground chicken
- ¼ cup fish sauce (I like Red Boat; see tip)

Directions

1. Heat 3 tablespoons of olive oil in a large skillet over medium heat. Add the spinach and sauté until wilted, about 2 minutes. Transfer the spinach to a medium bowl and let cool.
2. Once the spinach has cooled, add the chicken and fish sauce to it, and mix well with your hands. Form the mixture into 4 patties.
3. Heat the remaining 2 tablespoons of olive oil in the skillet over medium heat. Add the meat patties to the skillet and cook for about 4 minutes per side, or until browned and cooked through. Serve immediately or wrap and refrigerate for up to 1 week.

Nutritional Information: Calories: 351, Carbs: 4g, Fat: 27g, Fiber: 2g, Protein: 23g

Best Fried Chicken Ever

Serves: 4-6

Preparation time: 3 hours

Cooking time: 30 to 40 minutes

Ingredients

- 8 to 10 boneless, skin-on chicken thighs or boneless, skinless breasts (or a combo)
- 1 cup dill pickle juice
- ¾ cup almond flour
- 2 tablespoons minced garlic
- 2 teaspoons freshly ground black pepper
- 2 teaspoons paprika
- 1½ teaspoons salt
- 1 teaspoon dry mustard
- ¾ cup olive oil

Directions

1. In a large bowl or plastic bag, combine the chicken with the pickle juice and refrigerate for at least 3 hours or, ideally, overnight.
2. In a large bowl, combine the almond flour, garlic, pepper, paprika, salt, and dry mustard.
3. Heat the oil in a large skillet over medium-high heat.
4. While the oil is heating, remove the chicken from the marinade, shaking off any excess and discarding the marinade. Coat each piece of chicken in the flour mixture. Add the coated chicken to the skillet. Reduce the heat to medium-low and cook the chicken, turning it every 5 minutes or so, until it's browned and crispy, about 20 minutes.
5. Transfer the chicken to a paper towel–lined plate to drain. Serve hot.

Nutritional Information: Calories: 524, Carbs: 6g, Fat: 44g, Fiber: 3g, Protein: 26g

Chicken and Asparagus Curry

Serves: 4

Preparation time: 5 minutes

Cooking time: 15 minutes

Ingredients

- 1 tablespoon coconut oil
- ½ cup chopped onions
- 1 cinnamon stick
- 2 teaspoons ground fenugreek
- 2 teaspoons dry mustard
- 1 teaspoon ground cumin
- 2 boneless, skinless chicken thighs, cut into ½-inch pieces
- Fine sea salt and ground black pepper
- 1-pound asparagus, trimmed and cut into 2-inch pieces
- 1 (13½-ounce) can full-fat coconut milk
- ¼ cup chicken bone broth, homemade or store-bought
- 2 teaspoons Swerve confectioners'-style sweetener
- ½ teaspoon turmeric powder
- 1 tablespoon red curry paste
- Juice of 1 lime Fresh cilantro leaves, for garnish
- Lime wedges, for serving

Directions

1. Heat the oil in a cast-iron skillet over medium-high heat. Add the onions, cinnamon stick, fenugreek, dry mustard, and cumin and cook for 4 minutes or until the onions are soft.

2. Meanwhile, pat the chicken dry and season well on all sides with salt and pepper. Place in the skillet and cook for 5 minutes on each side, until the chicken is golden brown and no longer pink inside.

3. Add the asparagus, coconut milk, broth, sweetener, turmeric, curry paste, and lime juice. Stir well to combine. Bring to a simmer, then continue to simmer for 5 minutes or until the asparagus is cooked to your liking. Remove from the heat. Garnish with cilantro and serve with lime wedges.

4. Store in an airtight container in the refrigerator for up to 3 days. To reheat, place the curry in a saucepan over medium heat for a few minutes, until warmed to your liking.

Nutritional Information: Calories: 313, Carbs: 9g, Fat: 24g, Fiber: 3g, Protein: 15g

Chicken Tinga

Serves: 4

Preparation time: 10 minutes

Cooking time: 40 minutes

Ingredients

Chicken

- 1-pound bone-in, skin-on chicken thighs
- ¼ cup chopped onions 1 tablespoon minced garlic
- 1 tablespoon fine sea salt
- ½ tablespoon ground black pepper
- 4 ounces Mexican-style fresh (raw) chorizo, removed from casings
- ½ large white onion, chopped
- 1 clove garlic, minced
- 3 cups chopped tomatoes
- 1 cup husked and chopped tomatillos
- 2 tablespoons pureed chipotle
- 1½ teaspoons fine sea salt
- 1 teaspoon ground black pepper
- ½ teaspoon dried oregano leaves
- 1 sprig fresh marjoram 1 sprig fresh thyme
- ½ cup chicken bone broth, homemade or store-bought
- 1 batch Keto Tortillas (omit for egg-free), or 8 large lettuce leaves, for serving

Directions

1. Place the chicken, onions, garlic, salt, and pepper in a deep saucepan with 5 cups of water. Bring to a boil over high heat, then reduce the heat to medium and simmer for 20 minutes.

2. Remove the chicken to a cutting board. Using 2 forks, remove the chicken from the bones and shred it; discard the bones and set the shredded chicken aside.

3. Crumble the chorizo into a large cast-iron skillet. Place the skillet over medium heat, add the onion and garlic, and cook, stirring often, until the sausage is cooked through, about 5 minutes. Add the shredded chicken, tomatoes, tomatillos, chipotle, salt, pepper, and herbs. Continue cooking for 5 minutes, then add the chicken broth and cook for 5 more minutes. Remove the marjoram and thyme sprigs. Serve with tortillas or lettuce leaves.

4. Store in an airtight container in the refrigerator for up to 3 days. To reheat, place the chicken in a saucepan over medium heat for a few minutes, until warmed to your liking.

Nutritional Information: Calories: 506, Carbs: 10g, Fat: 33g, Fiber: 2g, Protein: 41g

Guacamole Lovers' Stuffed Chicken

Serves: 4

Preparation time: 10 minutes

Cooking time: 17 minutes

Ingredients

Guacamole

- 1 avocado, peeled and pitted 1
- ½ tablespoons lime juice, or more to taste
- 1 small plum tomato, diced
- ¼ cup finely diced onions
- 1 small clove garlic, smashed to a paste
- 1½ tablespoons chopped fresh cilantro leaves
- ¼ scant teaspoon fine sea salt
- ¼ scant teaspoon ground cumin
- 4 boneless, skinless chicken breast halves (about 2 pounds), pounded to ¼ inch thick 8 strips thin-cut bacon

For Serving

- Lime wedges Grape tomatoes
- 1 batch Pico de Gallo (optional)

Directions

1. Preheat the oven to 425°F.
2. Make the guacamole: Place the avocado and lime juice in a large bowl and mash until it reaches your desired consistency. Add the tomato, onions, garlic, cilantro, salt, and cumin and stir until well combined. Taste and add more lime juice, if desired. Place in a large resealable plastic bag, squeeze out all the air, and seal shut. (Note: If making the guacamole ahead of time, it will keep in the refrigerator for up to 3 days when stored this way.)

3. Place a chicken breast on a cutting board. Take a sharp knife and, holding it parallel to the chicken, make a 1-inch-wide incision at the top of the breast. Carefully cut into the breast to form a large pocket, leaving a ½-inch border along the sides and bottom. Repeat with the other 3 chicken breasts.

4. Cut a ¾-inch hole in one corner of the plastic bag with the guaca-mole, then squirt the guacamole into the pockets in the chicken breasts, dividing the guacamole evenly among them.

5. Wrap 2 strips of bacon around each chicken breast and secure the ends with toothpicks. Place the bacon-wrapped chicken on a rimmed baking sheet. Bake until the bacon is crisp and the chicken is cooked through, about 17 minutes. Serve with lime wedges, tomatoes, and pico de gallo, if desired.

6. Store in an airtight container in the refrigerator for up to 3 days. To reheat, place the chicken on a rimmed baking sheet in a preheated 400°F oven for 5 minutes or until warmed through.

Nutritional Information: Calories: 469, Carbs: 10g, Fat: 28g, Fiber: 4g, Protein: 45g

Chicken Meatball Marinara with Bean Sprouts and Broccoli

Serves: 6

Preparation time: 20 minutes

Cooking time: 45 minutes

Ingredients

- 1-pound ground chicken
- ¼ cup olive oil
- 2 cups chopped broccoli
- 1 (24-ounce) jar low-carb marinara sauce (I like Rao's Homemade)
- 1 (12-ounce) bag bean sprouts (see tip)

Directions

1. Form the ground chicken into 12 meatballs.
2. In a large skillet, heat the oil over medium-high heat. Add the meatballs and cook, turning occasionally, until browned, about 8 minutes. Add the broccoli and marinara sauce. Reduce the heat to low, cover, and let simmer for 30 minutes.
3. Add the bean sprouts, increase the heat to medium, and cook, uncovered, for 15 more minutes. Serve hot.

Nutritional Information: Calories: 247, Carbs: 10g, Fat: 15g, Fiber: 4g, Protein: 18g

Garlic Chicken Wings

Serves: 6

Preparation time: 10 minutes

Cooking time: 1 hour

Ingredients

- 24 frozen chicken wings
- 1 cup olive oil
- 6 garlic cloves, minced
- 1½ teaspoons salt
- 1 teaspoon freshly ground black pepper

Directions

1. Preheat the oven to 400°F. Place a baking rack on top of a large baking sheet.
2. In a large bowl, combine the frozen wings with the olive oil, garlic, salt, and pepper.
3. Arrange the chicken pieces on top of the baking rack on the baking sheet. Bake in the preheated oven for 1 hour, or until browned and crisp.

Nutritional Information: Calories: 880, Carbs: 1g, Fat: 76g, Fiber: 0g, Protein: 48g

Black Skillet Chicken Thighs with Artichoke Hearts

Serves: 6

Preparation time: 10 minutes

Cooking time: 50 Minutes

Ingredients

- 6 tablespoons olive oil
- 6 boneless, skin-on chicken thighs
- 1 (14-ounce) can artichoke hearts, drained
- 1 onion, diced
- ½ cup bone broth
- 1 teaspoon salt
- 1 teaspoon freshly ground black pepper
- Juice of 1 lemon

Directions

1. Preheat the oven to 400°F.
2. Heat the olive oil in a large cast iron skillet over medium-high heat. Add the chicken and cook until nicely browned on the bottom, about 4 minutes.
3. Once browned, flip the chicken over and add the artichokes, onion, broth, salt, and pepper.
4. Place the skillet in the preheated oven and cook for 40 minutes, or until the chicken is cooked through.
5. Remove the skillet from the oven and squeeze the lemon juice over the top. Serve hot.

Nutritional Information: Calories: 479, Carbs: 6g, Fat: 39g, Fiber: 4g, Protein: 25g

Jenny Pale

Sheet Pan BBQ Chicken Breasts

Serves: 8

Preparation time: 8 minutes

Cooking time: 25 Minutes

Ingredients

- 4 boneless, skinless chicken breast halves (about 2 pounds), sliced into 1½ by 4-inch strips
- ½ cup Simple BBQ Sauce
- 3 firm and barely ripe avocados
- 1 (1-pound) package thin-cut bacon (about 20 strips)

Directions

1. Preheat the oven to 425F. Line a rimmed baking sheet with parchment paper.
2. Baste the chicken strips with BBQ sauce.
3. Peel and pit the avocados, then slice into thick fry shapes. Wrap each slice with a strip of bacon and secure with a toothpick.
4. Place the chicken and bacon-wrapped avocado slices on the lined baking sheet. Bake for 20 to 25 minutes, until the avocados are tender and the juice of the chicken runs clear when the center of the thickest part is cut and the internal temperature is at least 165°F. 5.
5. Store in an airtight container in the refrigerator for up to 3 days or in the freezer for up to a month. To reheat, place the chicken and fries on a baking sheet in a preheated 375°F oven for 5 minutes or until warmed through.

Nutritional Information: Calories: 464, Carbs: 7g, Fat: 40g, Fiber: 23g, Protein: 23g

Chicken with Dried Beef

Serves: 12

Preparation time: 20 minutes

Cooking time: 1 hour

Ingredients

- 6 large boneless, skinless chicken breasts, each cut in half
- 1 (2-ounce) jar or can dried beef
- 12 strips bacon
- 1¼ cups bone broth
- 1 (8-ounce) container dairy-free cream cheese with chives (such as Kite Hill)
- 1 celery stalk, diced
- ½ cup canned coconut milk
- 1 teaspoon freshly ground black pepper

Directions

1. Preheat the oven to 375°F.
2. Wrap each piece of chicken with 2 pieces of dried beef, and then with 1 slice of bacon. Arrange the wrapped chicken pieces in a baking dish.
3. In a medium bowl, mix together the broth, cream cheese, celery, coconut milk, and pepper. Pour the mixture over the chicken pieces.
4. Bake, uncovered, in the preheated oven for 1 hour, or until the chicken is cooked through.

Nutritional Information: Calories: 309, Carbs: 2g, Fat: 21g, Fiber: 0g, Protein: 28g

Chili-Garlic Chicken with Broccoli

Serves: 6

Preparation time: 10 minutes

Cooking time: 6 hours

Ingredients

- 6 boneless, skinless chicken breasts (about 1¼ pounds total), cut into bite-size pieces
- 1 head broccoli, chopped
- 8 ounces whole mushrooms
- 1 large onion, diced
- 2 cups bone broth
- ½ cup coconut aminos
- 5 tablespoons chili-garlic sauce
- ¼ cup avocado oil
- 2 tablespoons fish sauce (such as Red Boat)
- 1 teaspoon minced garlic
- ½ teaspoon grated fresh ginger

Directions

1. In a slow cooker, combine the chicken, broccoli, mushrooms, onion, bone broth, coconut aminos, chili-garlic sauce, avocado oil, fish sauce, garlic, and ginger.
2. Cover and cook on low for 6 hours. Serve hot.

Nutritional information: Calories: 244, Carbs: 9g, Fat: 11g, Fiber: 0g, Protein: 29g

Poppy Seed Chicken

Serves: 8

Preparation time: 20 minutes

Cooking time: 45 minutes

Ingredients

- 2 tablespoons olive oil, plus more for greasing the baking dish
- 6 boneless, skinless chicken breasts (about 2 pounds), cooked and shredded
- 1 (8-ounce) container dairy-free cream cheese (such as Kite Hill)
- 1 cup bone broth 8 ounces mushrooms, sliced
- 1 14-ounce can coconut milk
- 2 tablespoons olive oil
- 1½ teaspoons garlic salt
- 2 tablespoons poppy seeds
- ¼ cup slivered almonds

Directions

1. Preheat the oven to 350°F. Grease a 9-by-13-inch baking dish.
2. Arrange the shredded chicken in an even layer in the prepared baking dish.
3. In a medium saucepan over low heat, soften the cream cheese, stirring constantly. Once the cheese is melted, stir in the bone broth, mushrooms, coconut milk, olive oil, and garlic salt.
4. Continue cooking on low until the sauce is well combined and thickened. Remove from the heat and stir in the poppy seeds. Immediately pour the sauce over the shredded chicken in the baking dish. Sprinkle the almonds over the top and bake in the preheated oven for 40 minutes, or until bubbly.

Nutritional Information: Calories 374, Carbs: 7g, Fat: 26g, Fiber: 1g, Protein: 29g

Jenny Pale

Curry Braised Chicken Legs

Serves: 8

Preparation time: 10 minutes

Cooking time: 45 minutes

Ingredients

- ¼ cup avocado oil or coconut oil
- ¼ cup diced onions
- 1 tablespoon peeled and grated fresh ginger
- 1 tablespoon minced garlic
- 1 cup sliced button mushrooms
- 8 chicken legs
- 1 teaspoon fine sea salt
- 1 cup chicken bone broth, homemade or store-bought
- ½ cup full-fat coconut milk
- 2 tablespoons red curry paste
- 2 tablespoons lime juice Sliced scallions, for garnish
- Lime wedges, for serving

Directions

1. Heat the oil in a large cast-iron skillet over medium-high heat. Add the onions and cook for 2 minutes or until soft. Add the ginger and garlic and cook for another minute. Add the mushrooms and sauté until golden brown, about 2 minutes.

2. Season the chicken on all sides with the salt. Place the chicken in the skillet and sear on all sides for about 2 minutes per side, until golden brown. Add the broth, coconut milk, and curry paste and whisk to combine. Cover and cook for 30 to 40 minutes, until the chicken is cooked through and fork-tender; during cooking, lift the lid occasionally and stir to deglaze the bottom of the pan.

3. Stir in the lime juice. Taste and add more salt, if desired. Garnish with scallions and serve with lime wedges.

4. Store in an airtight container in the refrigerator for up to 3 days or in the freezer for up to a month. To reheat, place the chicken in a skillet over medium heat, cover, and cook until warmed through, about 5 minutes.

Nutritional Information: Calories 363, Carbs: 2g, Fat: 25g, Fiber: 0.5g, Protein: 30g

Turkey Rissoles

Serves: 4

Preparation time: 10 minutes

Cooking time: 25 minutes

Ingredients

- 1 pound ground turkey
- 1 scallion, white and green parts, finely chopped
- 1 teaspoon minced garlic
- Pinch sea salt
- Pinch freshly ground black pepper
- 1 cup ground almonds
- 2 tablespoons olive oil

Directions

1. Preheat the oven to 350°F. Line a baking sheet with aluminum foil and set aside.
2. In a medium bowl, mix together the turkey, scallion, garlic, salt, and pepper until well combined.
3. Shape the turkey mixture into 8 patties and flatten them out.
4. Place the ground almonds in a shallow bowl and dredge the turkey patties in the ground almonds to coat.
5. Place a large skillet over medium heat and add the olive oil.
6. Brown the turkey patties on both sides, about 10 minutes in total.
7. Transfer the patties to the baking sheet and bake them until cooked through, flipping them once, about 15 minutes in total.

Nutritional Information: Calories 440, Carbs: 7g, Fat: 34g, Fiber: 4g, Protein: 27g

Chicken and Mushroom Kabobs

Serves: 2

Preparation time: 10 minutes

Cooking time: 12 minutes

Ingredients

Marinade

- ½ cup MCT oil, avocado oil, or extra-virgin olive oil
- 3 tablespoons lime juice
- 1 tablespoon chopped fresh tarragon or parsley
- 1 teaspoon chopped fresh oregano
- 1 teaspoon fine sea salt
- 1 teaspoon ground black pepper
- 3 cloves garlic, minced
- 2 boneless, skinless chicken thighs, cut into ½-inch pieces
- 6 large button mushrooms, cut into quarters

Dipping Sauce:

- ¼ cup mayonnaise, homemade or store-bought
- 1 tablespoon lime juice
- 1 tablespoon sliced fresh chives, or 2 teaspoons dried chives
- Fine sea salt and ground black pepper

Special Equipment

- 6 wood skewers, soaked in water for 15 minutes

Directions

1. Place the ingredients for the marinade in a large bowl and stir to combine. Add the chicken and stir well to coat. Cover and refrigerate for at least 3 hours or overnight.

2. Preheat a grill to high heat. Thread a piece of marinated chicken onto a skewer, followed by a mushroom quarter. Repeat 3 more times to fill the skewer. Then repeat with the remaining skewers, chicken, and mushrooms. Discard the marinade.

3. Lightly brush the hot grill grate with oil, then place the kabobs on the grill and cook for 6 minutes. Flip and grill for another 6 minutes or until the chicken is cooked through.

4. Meanwhile, prepare the dipping sauce: Place the mayonnaise, lime juice, and chives in a small food processor or blender and blend until smooth. Season to taste with salt and pepper.

5. Place the kabobs on a platter and serve with a bowl of the dipping sauce on the side.

6. Store leftover kabobs and sauce in separate airtight containers in the refrigerator for up to 4 days; the kabobs can be frozen for up to a month. Reheat the kabobs in a lightly greased skillet for 2 minutes per side or until warmed to your liking.

Nutritional Information: Calories 436, Carbs: 6g, Fat: 36g, Fiber: 0.5g, Protein: 24g

Easy Asian Chicken Legs

Serves: 4

Preparation time: 5 minutes

Cooking time: 35 minutes

Ingredients

- ½ cup chicken bone broth, homemade or store-bought
- ⅓ cup Swerve confectioners
- ⅓ cup wheat-free tamari
- ¼ cup tomato sauce
- 1 tablespoon coconut vinegar or apple cider vinegar
- ¾ teaspoon crushed red pepper
- ¼ teaspoon peeled and grated fresh ginger
- 1 clove garlic, smashed to a paste
- 5 drops orange oil (optional)
- 1-pound bone-in, skin-on chicken legs or thighs

For Garnish:

- 1 lime, quartered
- 1 tablespoon toasted sesame seeds
- 4 scallions, sliced Fresh cilantro leaves

Directions

1. Preheat the oven to 400°F.
2. Place the broth, sweetener, tamari, tomato sauce, vinegar, crushed red pepper, ginger, garlic, and orange oil, if using, in a small bowl. Stir well, then pour half of the sauce into another bowl and set aside for serving.
3. Place the chicken in an 8-inch square baking dish and baste with the other half of the sauce. Cover and bake for 25 minutes. Uncover and bake for

another 10 minutes or until the chicken is cooked through and no longer pink inside.

4. Serve the chicken with the reserved sauce. Garnish with lime quarters, toasted sesame seeds, sliced scallions, and cilantro leaves.

5. Store in an airtight container in the refrigerator for up to 4 days or in the freezer for up to a month. To reheat, place the chicken in a preheated 375°F oven for 10 minutes or until warmed to your liking.

Nutritional Information: Calories 322, Carbs: 6g, Fat: 25g, Fiber: 2g, Protein: 33g

Lemon Pepper Chicken Tender

Serves: 4

Preparation time: 7 minutes

Cooking time: 20 minutes

Ingredients

- ¼ cup avocado oil or melted coconut oil
- 1 tablespoon minced garlic
- 2 lemons, divided
- 4 boneless, skinless chicken breast halves (about 2 pounds), cut into 1-inch-wide strips
- 2 tablespoons lemon pepper seasoning
- 2 teaspoons fine sea salt
- 1 teaspoon black peppercorns, for garnish
- Chopped fresh parsley or oregano, for garnish

Directions

1. Preheat the oven to 400°F.
2. Make the lemon sauce: Place the oil and garlic in a small bowl. Grate the zest of one of the lemons and add 2 teaspoons of the zest to the bowl. Juice the zested lemon and add the juice to the bowl. Stir well.
3. Cut the second lemon into thin slices. Arrange the slices on a rimmed baking sheet or a 13 by 9-inch baking dish.
4. Season all sides of the chicken strips with the lemon pepper seasoning and salt. Place on top of the lemon slices and drizzle with the lemon sauce.
5. Bake for 18 to 20 minutes, until the chicken is no longer pink inside. Serve garnished with peppercorns and fresh parsley.
6. Store in an airtight container in the refrigerator for up to 3 days or in the freezer for up to a month. To reheat, place the chicken on a rimmed baking sheet in a preheated 375°F oven for 5 minutes or until warmed through.

Nutritional Information: Calories 432, Carbs: 6g, Fat: 25g, Fiber: 2g, Protein: 44g

Paprika Chicken

Serves: 4

Preparation time: 10 minutes

Cooking time: 25 minutes

Ingredients

- 4 (4-ounce) chicken breasts, skin-on
- Sea salt
- Freshly ground black pepper
- 1 tablespoon olive oil
- ½ cup chopped sweet onion
- ½ cup heavy (whipping) cream
- 2 teaspoons smoked paprika
- ½ cup sour cream
- 2 tablespoons chopped fresh parsley

Directions

1. Lightly season the chicken with salt and pepper.
2. Place a large skillet over medium-high heat and add the olive oil.
3. Sear the chicken on both sides until almost cooked through, about 15 minutes in total. Remove the chicken to a plate.
4. Add the onion to the skillet and sauté until tender, about 4 minutes.
5. Stir in the cream and paprika and bring the liquid to a simmer.
6. Return the chicken and any accumulated juices to the skillet and simmer the chicken for 5 minutes until completely cooked.
7. Stir in the sour cream and remove the skillet from the heat.
8. Serve topped with the parsley.

Nutritional Information: Calories 389, Carbs: 4g, Fat: 30g, Fiber: 0g, Protein: 25g

Bundt Pan Chicken

Serves: 8

Preparation time: 7 minutes

Cooking time: 45 minutes

Ingredients

- 2 medium zucchini, sliced ½ inch thick (about 2½ cups)
- ½ small onion, cut into 1-inch pieces
- 1 tablespoon plus 1 teaspoon minced garlic
- 4 teaspoons fine sea salt, divided
- 2 teaspoons ground black pepper, divided
- 4 tablespoons avocado oil or melted lard, duck fat, or bacon fat, divided
- 3 sprigs fresh thyme, divided
- 1 (3-pound) whole chicken

Directions

1. Place all of the oven racks in the lower portion of the oven. (The chicken stands tall and needs a lot of space above it.) Preheat the oven to 425°F.
2. Place the zucchini, onion, and garlic in a medium-sized bowl. Season with 3 teaspoons of the salt and 1½ teaspoons of the pepper. Drizzle with 1 tablespoon of the oil and toss to coat well. Place in the Bundt pan. Top with a thyme sprig.
3. Place a piece of aluminum foil over the hole of the Bundt pan, then place parchment paper over the foil so the food doesn't touch the foil while roasting.
4. Pat the chicken dry and use your hands to rub the remaining 3 tablespoons of oil all over the outside. Season the inside and outside of the chicken well with the remaining teaspoon of salt and remaining ½ teaspoon of pepper. Place the remaining 2 sprigs of thyme inside the cavity.

5. Place the chicken in the middle of the Bundt pan with the neck facing up. Roast in the oven for 45 minutes or until the chicken is cooked through and the juices run clear. Serve with the roasted veggies.

6. Store in an airtight container in the refrigerator for up to 3 days or in the freezer for up to a month. To reheat, place on a rimmed baking sheet in a preheated 375°F oven for 8 minutes or until warmed through.

Nutritional Information: Calories 445, Carbs: 6g, Fat: 33g, Fiber: 1g, Protein: 33g

Coconut Chicken

Serves: 4

Preparation time: 15 minutes

Cooking time: 25 minutes

Ingredients

- 2 tablespoons olive oil
- 4 (4-ounce) chicken breasts, cut into 2-inch chunks
- ½ cup chopped sweet onion
- 1 cup coconut milk
- 1 tablespoon curry powder
- 1 teaspoon ground cumin
- 1 teaspoon ground coriander
- ¼ cup chopped fresh cilantro

Directions

1. Place a large saucepan over medium-high heat and add the olive oil.
2. Sauté the chicken until almost cooked through, about 10 minutes.
3. Add the onion and sauté for an additional 3 minutes.
4. In a medium bowl, whisk together the coconut milk, curry powder, cumin, and coriander.
5. Pour the sauce into the saucepan with the chicken and bring the liquid to a boil.
6. Reduce the heat and simmer until the chicken is tender and the sauce has thickened, about 10 minutes.
7. Serve the chicken with the sauce, topped with cilantro.

Nutritional Information: Calories 382, Carbs: 5g, Fat: 31g, Fiber: 1g, Protein: 23g

Jenny Pale

Chapter Eight: Beef & Pork Recipes

Dinner Roast with Vegetables

Serves: 8

Preparation time: 15 minutes

Cooking time: 8 to 10 hours

Ingredients

- 1 (3-pound) chuck roast
- 1 bunch radishes (about 12), diced
- 2 cups bone broth
- 5 celery stalks, chopped
- 8 ounces mushrooms, diced
- 1 onion, diced
- ¼ cup coconut aminos
- ½ cup dairy-free ranch dressing (such as Tessemae's)

Directions

1. In a slow cooker, combine the chuck roast, radishes, bone broth, celery, mushrooms, onion, coconut aminos, and ranch dressing.
2. Cover and cook on low for 8 to 10 hours, or until the meat can be easily pulled apart with a fork.

Nutritional Information: Calories 383, Carbs: 4g, Fat: 18g, Fiber: 1g, Protein: 47g

Beef Liver Burgers

Serves: 5

Preparation time: 10 minutes

Cooking time: 20 minutes

Ingredients

- 1-pound ground beef or bison
- 8 ounces beef liver, cut into small pieces
- 3 tablespoons sugar-free ketchup (such as Primal Kitchen)
- 3 teaspoons garlic salt, divided
- 3 tablespoons olive oil

Directions

1. In a small bowl, combine the ground meat, liver, ketchup, and 2 teaspoons of garlic salt. Mix well and form into 4 to 6 burger patties.
2. In a cast iron skillet, heat the oil over medium heat. Add the burgers, then sprinkle them with the remaining teaspoon of garlic salt. Cook for 8 to 10 minutes per side, or until cooked through. Serve hot.

Nutritional Information: Calories 497, Carbs: 3g, Fat: 41g, Fiber: 0g, Protein: 30g

Easy BBQ Brisket

Serves: 8

Preparation time: 4 minutes

Cooking time: 4 hours

Ingredients

- 4 pounds brisket
- 6 tablespoons powdered sweetener
- 2 tablespoons fine sea salt
- 1 tablespoon garlic powder
- 1 tablespoon ground black pepper
- 1 tablespoon onion powder
- 1 tablespoon dry mustard
- 1 ½ cups tomato sauce
- 1 ½ cups beef bone broth, homemade
- 2 teaspoons liquid smoke
- Chopped fresh parsley, for garnish

Directions

1. Pat the brisket dry. Place in a large roasting pan that snugly fits the brisket and allow it to sit at room temperature for 10 to 15 minutes.
2. Preheat oven to 350F,
3. Place the sweetener, salt, pepper, garlic powder, onion powder, and dry mustard in a small bowl and stir to combine. Sprinkle the mixture all over the brisket, then use your hands to rub it into the meat.

5. Place the brisket in the oven and cook, uncovered, for 1 hour

6. Meanwhile, place the tomato sauce, broth and liquid smoke in a medium-sized bowl. Stir well to combine

7. Remove the brisket from the oven and add the tomato-broth mixture to the pan. Lower the oven temperature to 300F, cover the pan, and slow cook the brisket for 2 ½ hours or until fork-tender. If the brisket isn't tender enough after 2 ½ hours, cook, covered, for an additional 30 minutes.

8. Allow the meat to rest on a cutting board for 10 minutes while you make sauce. Pour the juices from the roasting pan into a saucepan and boil for 7 minutes or until thickened to your liking.

9. Slice the meat across the grain into 1/8-inch slices. Serves with the sauce. Garnish with parsley, if desired.

10. Store in an airtight container in the refrigerator for up to 3 days. To reheat, place the brisket on a rimmed baking sheet in a preheated 350F oven for 5 minutes or until warmed through.

Nutritional Information: Calories 543, Carbs: 4g, Fat: 40g, Fiber: 1g, Protein: 39g

Lamb Chops With Kalamata Tapenade

Serves: 4

Preparation time: 15 minutes

Cooking time: 25 minutes

Ingredients

For the Tapenade

- 1 cup pitted Kalamata olives
- 2 tablespoons chopped fresh parsley
- 2 tablespoons extra-virgin olive oil
- 2 teaspoons minced garlic
- 2 teaspoons freshly squeezed lemon juice

For the Lamb Chops

- 2 (1-pound) racks French-cut lamb chops (8 bones each)
- Sea salt
- Freshly ground black pepper
- 1 tablespoon olive oil

Directions

1. Place the olives, parsley, olive oil, garlic, and lemon juice in a food processor and process until the mixture is puréed but still slightly chunky.
2. Transfer the tapenade to a container and store sealed in the refrigerator until needed.

To Make the Lamb Chops

1. Preheat the oven to 450°F.
2. Season the lamb racks with salt and pepper.
3. Place a large ovenproof skillet over medium-high heat and add the olive oil.

4. Pan sear the lamb racks on all sides until browned, about 5 minutes in total.

5. Arrange the racks upright in the skillet, with the bones interlaced, and roast them in the oven until they reach your desired doneness, about 20 minutes for medium-rare or until the internal temperature reaches 125°F.

6. Let the lamb rest for 10 minutes and then cut the lamb racks into chops. Arrange 4 chops per person on the plate and top with the Kalamata tapenade.

Directions: Calories 348, Carbs: 2g, Fat: 28g, Fiber: 1g, Protein: 21g

Rosemary-Garlic Lamb Racks

Serves: 4

Preparation time: 10 minutes + 1 hour Marinating Time

Cooking time: 25 minutes

Ingredients

- 4 tablespoons extra-virgin olive oil
- 2 tablespoons finely chopped fresh rosemary
- 2 teaspoons minced garlic
- Pinch sea salt
- 2 (1-pound) racks French-cut lamb chops (8 bones each)

Directions

1. In a small bowl, whisk together the olive oil, rosemary, garlic, and salt.
2. Place the racks in a sealable freezer bag and pour the olive oil mixture into the bag. Massage the meat through the bag so it is coated with the marinade. Press the air out of the bag and seal it.
3. Marinate the lamb racks in the refrigerator for 1 to 2 hours.
4. Preheat the oven to 450°F.
5. Place a large ovenproof skillet over medium-high heat. Take the lamb racks out of the bag and sear them in the skillet on all sides, about 5 minutes in total.
6. Arrange the racks upright in the skillet, with the bones interlaced, and roast them in the oven until they reach your desired doneness, about 20 minutes for medium-rare or until the internal temperature reaches 125°F.
7. Let the lamb rest for 10 minutes and then cut the racks into chops.
8. Serve 4 chops per person.

Nutritional Information: Calories 354, Carbs: 0g, Fat: 30g, Fiber: 0g, Protein: 21g

Jenny Pale

Philly Cheeses Teak Bake
Serves: 8

Preparation time: 10 minutes

Cooking time: 30 minutes

Ingredients

- 2 tablespoons olive oil, plus more for greasing the baking dish
- 1 (8-ounce) container dairy-free cream cheese (such as Kite Hill)
- ¾ cup sugar-free mayonnaise (such as Primal Kitchen)
- ¼ cup canned coconut milk or nut milk
- ¼ cup whole-grain mustard
- 2 tablespoons minced garlic
- 2 tablespoons olive oil
- 1 tomato, chopped
- 1 green bell pepper, seeded and chopped
- 1 onion, diced
- 8 ounces mushrooms, chopped
- 1½ pounds deli-sliced roast beef, chopped

Directions

1. Preheat the oven to 400°F. Grease a 9-by-13-inch baking dish.
2. In a medium bowl, stir together the cream cheese, mayonnaise, coconut milk, mustard, and garlic until well combined.
3. Heat the olive oil in a large skillet over medium heat. Add the tomato, green pepper, onion, and mushrooms. Cook, stirring frequently, until the vegetables are softened, about 8 minutes.

4. Spread the roast beef in an even layer in the prepared baking dish. Top with the vegetable mixture and then the cream cheese mixture. Bake in the preheated oven for 20 minutes, or until the dish is hot and bubbly.

Nutritional Information: Calories 534, Carbs: 5g, Fat: 42g, Fiber: 2g, Protein: 34g

Secret Seasoning Sirloin Steak

Serves: 2

Preparation time: 5 minutes

Cooking time: 20 minutes

Ingredients

- 2 (6- to 8-ounce) sirloin steaks, at room temperature
- ¼ cup sugar-free ketchup (such as Primal Kitchen)
- 4 teaspoons garlic salt
- ¼ cup olive oil

Directions

1. Heat the broiler to high.
2. Lay out the steaks on a plate and cover each side with the ketchup and garlic salt.
3. In a cast iron skillet, heat the oil over high heat. Add the steaks and cook for 1 minute on each side.
4. Transfer the skillet to the broiler and cook for 5 minutes more.
5. Remove the skillet from the oven, flip the steaks over, and let them continue to cook in the hot pan for 10 more minutes.
6. Serve immediately.

Nutritional Information: Calories 462, Carbs: 3g, Fat: 34g, Fiber: 2g, Protein: 36g

Slopy Joes

Serves: 4

Preparation time: 10 minutes

Cooking time: 30 minutes

Ingredients

- 1-pound ground beef
- 1 onion, diced
- ¾ cup sugar-free ketchup (such as Primal Kitchen)
- 2 tablespoons garlic powder
- 1 tablespoon white vinegar
- 1 tablespoon
- Swerve granular (or another granulated alternative sweetener)

Directions

1. Heat a large skillet over medium-high heat. Add the meat and cook, stirring, until it begins to brown, about 3 minutes. Add the onion and cook, stirring frequently, until the meat is browned, and the onion is softened, about 5 minutes.
2. Stir in the ketchup, garlic powder, vinegar, and sweetener. Reduce the heat to medium-low and cook for 20 minutes more. Serve hot.

Nutritional Information: Calories 356, Carbs: 4g, Fat: 28g, Fiber: 1g, Protein: 19g

Curry Short Ribs

Serves: 4

Preparation time: 5 minutes

Cooking time: 8 hours

Ingredients

- ¼ cup chopped onions
- ¼ cup curry powder
- 1 cup beef bone broth, homemade or store-bought
- 2 tablespoons swerve confectioners
- 1 tablespoon lime juice
- 2 cloves garlic, minced
- 4 beef short ribs (2 pounds total)

For Garnish

- Sliced scallions
- Chopped fresh cilantro

Directions

1. Place the broth, onions, curry powder, sweetener, lime juice, and garlic in a 6-quart slow cooker and stir well to combine.
2. Add the ribs and cook, covered, on a low for 7 to 8 hours or until the meat is tender and easily pulls away from the bone
3. To create a thicker, pour the sauce from the slow cooker into a saucepan and boil while whisking for 2 minutes or until thickened to your liking. Taste and add more salt or lime juice, if desired.
4. Serve the ribs with the sauce. Garnish with scallions and cilantro
5. Store in an airtight container in the refrigerator for up to 4 days. To reheat, place the ribs on a rimmed baking sheet in a preheated 400F oven for a few minutes, until warmed to your liking

Nutritional Information: Calories 528, Carbs: 4g, Fat: 47g, Fiber: 0.1g, Protein: 24g

Lamb Leg with Sun-Dried Tomato Pesto

Serves: 8

Preparation time: 15 minutes

Cooking time: 70 hours

Ingredients

For the Pesto

- 1 cup sun-dried tomatoes packed in oil, drained
- ¼ cup pine nuts
- 2 tablespoons extra-virgin olive oil
- 2 tablespoons chopped fresh basil
- 2 teaspoons minced garlic

For the Lamb Leg

- 1 (2-pound) lamb leg
- Sea salt Freshly ground black pepper
- 2 tablespoons olive oil

To Make The Pesto

1. Place the sun-dried tomatoes, pine nuts, olive oil, basil, and garlic in a blender or food processor; process until smooth.
2. Set aside until needed.

To Make the Lamb Leg

1. Preheat the oven to 400°F.
2. Season the lamb leg all over with salt and pepper.
3. Place a large ovenproof skillet over medium-high heat and add the olive oil.
4. Sear the lamb on all sides until nicely browned, about 6 minutes in total.

5. Spread the sun-dried tomato pesto all over the lamb and place the lamb on a baking sheet. Roast until the meat reaches your desired doneness, about 1 hour for medium.

6. Let the lamb rest for 10 minutes before slicing and serving.

Nutritional Information: Calories 352, Carbs: 3g, Fat: 29g, Fiber: 2g, Protein: 5g

Fajita Kabobs

Serves: 4

Preparation time: 10 minutes

Cooking time: 6 minutes

Ingredients

- ¼ cup lime juice
- ¼ avocado oil
- 2 cloves garlic, minced
- 1 teaspoon fine sea salt
- ¾ cayenne pepper
- 1 teaspoon chili powder
- ½ teaspoon paprika
- ½ teaspoon ground cumin
- 2 (8-ounce) boneless rib-eye steaks, about 1 inch thick
- 8 grape tomatoes
- 1 red onion
- 2 green bell peppers
- ½ cup Citrus Avocado salsa, for serving
- Boston lettuce leaves, for serving

Directions

1. Make the marinade: Place the oil, lime juice, garlic, salt, and spices in a large bowl
2. Cut the steaks into 1-inch cubes. Add the meat to marinade and stir to coat well. Cover and refrigerate for at least 1 hour or overnight
3. Preheat a grill to high heat. While the grill is heating up, cut the bell peppers and onion into 1-inch squares. Remove the meat from the marinade; reserve the marinade for basting.

4. Place 2 cubes of steak on a skewer, followed by an onion piece, a steak piece, a bell pepper piece, a steak piece, and a grape tomato, then repeat the sequence with another piece of steak, then onion, steak, and bell pepper, ending with 2 pieces of steak. Repeat with the remaining skewers and ingredients.

5. Lightly brush the hot grill grates with oil. Place the skewers on the grill for 3 minutes, basting every minute with the reserved marinade. Flip and cook, basting, for another 3 minutes for medium-rare steak.

6. Serve with salsa and lettuce leaves for wrapping, if desired

7. Store in an airtight container in the refrigerator for up to 4 days. To reheat, place in a skillet over medium heat, stirring often, for a few minutes, until warmed to your liking.

Nutritional Information: Calories 370, Carbs: 10g, Fat: 28g, Fiber: 2g, Protein: 21g

Cabbage Slaw with Ground Beef

Serves: 4

Preparation time: 5 minutes

Cooking time: 30 minutes

Ingredients

- 3 tablespoons olive oil
- 1-pound ground beef
- 1 (16-ounce) bag cabbage slaw mix
- 3 tablespoons coconut aminos
- 1 tablespoon fish sauce (such as Red Boat)

Directions

1. Heat the olive oil in a large skillet over medium-high heat. Add the meat and cook, stirring, until browned, about 7 minutes. Add the cabbage and cook, stirring occasionally, until wilted, about 15 minutes.
2. Stir in the coconut aminos and fish sauce, and simmer for 5 minutes more.
3. Serve hot or cover and store in the refrigerator for up to 5 days.

Nutritional Information: Calories 463, Carbs: 10g, Fat: 39g, Fiber: 1g, Protein: 18g

Bacon-Wrapped Beef Tenderloin

Serves: 4

Preparation time: 10 minutes

Cooking time: 15 minutes

Ingredients

- 4 (4-ounce) beef tenderloin steaks
- Sea salt
- Freshly ground black pepper
- 8 bacon slices
- 1 tablespoon extra-virgin olive oil

Directions

1. Preheat the oven to 450°F.
2. Season the steaks with salt and pepper.
3. Wrap each steak snugly around the edges with 2 slices of bacon and secure the bacon with toothpicks.
4. Place a large skillet over medium-high heat and add the olive oil.
5. Pan sear the steaks for 4 minutes per side and transfer them to a baking sheet.
6. Roast the steaks until they reach your desired doneness, about 6 minutes for medium.
7. Remove the steaks from the oven and let them rest for 10 minutes.
8. Remove the toothpicks and serve.

Nutritional Information: Calories 565, Carbs: 0g, Fat: 49g, Fiber: 0g, Protein: 28g

Cheese Burger Hash

Serves: 10

Preparation time: 20 minutes

Cooking time: 50 minutes

Ingredients

- 3 tablespoons olive oil, plus more for greasing the baking dish
- 2 pounds ground beef
- 1 (16-ounce) bag cabbage slaw mix
- 1 large onion, diced
- 8 ounces mushrooms, sliced
- 1 (8-ounce) container dairy-free cream cheese with chives (such as Kite Hill)
- 1 cup canned coconut milk
- 3 tablespoons nutritional yeast
- 2 teaspoons granulated garlic
- 1 teaspoon salt
- 1 teaspoon freshly ground black pepper
- 1 batch Perfect Bacon, crumbled

Directions

1. Preheat the oven to 350°F. Grease a 9-by-13-inch baking dish.
2. Heat the oil in a large skillet over medium-high heat. Add the meat, cabbage slaw mix, onion, and mushrooms, and cook, stirring frequently, for 15 to 20 minutes, or until the meat is browned and the vegetables are softened.
3. Transfer the mixture to the prepared baking dish.
4. In a large microwave-safe bowl, heat the cream cheese for 40 seconds in the microwave to soften.

5. To the bowl with the cream cheese, add the coconut milk, nutritional yeast, garlic, salt, and pepper, and whisk to combine well.

6. Pour the cream cheese mixture over the meat and vegetables in the baking dish. Bake in the preheated oven for 30 minutes, or until bubbling and lightly browned on top. 7Serve hot, topped with the bacon.

Nutritional Information: Calories 557, Carbs: 9g, Fat: 45g, Fiber: 4g, Protein: 29g

Kielbasa and Sauerkraut

Serves: 4

Preparation time: 5 minutes

Cooking time: 10 minutes

Ingredients

- 1 (16-ounce) jar or can sauerkraut
- 1-pound pork kielbasa, diced
- 2 tablespoons olive oil

Directions

1. In a medium saucepan, bring the sauerkraut to a boil over medium-high heat. Add the diced sausage and the olive oil, and simmer over low heat until heated through, about 5 minutes.

Nutritional Information: Calories 435, Carbs: 6g, Fat: 39g, Fiber: 3g, Protein: 29g

Potluck BBQ Pork

Serves: 7

Preparation time: 10 minutes

Cooking time: 8 hours

Ingredients

- 1 (2-pound) whole pork shoulder
- 2 (6-ounce) cans tomato paste
- 1 white onion, diced
- 1 cup low-carb tomato sauce
- 1 batch Red Pepper Dry Rub
- 3 tablespoons white vinegar
- 2 tablespoons coconut aminos
- 2 tablespoons whole-grain mustard

Directions

1. In a large slow cooker, combine the pork, tomato paste, onion, tomato sauce, dry rub, vinegar, coconut aminos, and mustard.
2. Cover and cook on low for 8 hours.
3. Once cooked, remove the meat and shred it using a hand mixer or two forks. Return the meat to the pot and stir to mix well. Serve hot.

Nutritional Information: Calories 342, Carbs: 10g, Fat: 22g, Fiber: 4g, Protein: 29g

Jenny Pale

Garlic Pork Chops with Onion-And-Mushroom Gravy
Serves: 4

Preparation time: 10 minutes

Cooking time: 1 hour

Ingredients

- ¼ cup garlic powder
- 1 teaspoon salt
- 1 teaspoon freshly ground black pepper
- ½ teaspoon cayenne
- 4 pork chops
- ¼ cup olive oil
- 8 ounces whole mushrooms
- 1 onion, diced
- 2 cups bone broth
- ¼ cup coconut milk

Directions

1. In a small bowl, mix together the garlic powder, salt, pepper, and cayenne.
2. Coat the pork chops with the spice rub mixture, using all of the mixture.
3. Heat the oil in a large cast iron skillet over medium heat. Add the mushrooms and onion and cook, stirring frequently, until softened, about 8 minutes. Add the broth and cook for 20 minutes, or until the liquid is reduced by about half.
4. Increase the heat to high and add the pork chops. Cook for 8 to 10 minutes on each side, depending on the thickness of the pork chop, or until browned and cooked through.
5. Remove the chops from the skillet, but continue to cook the vegetables in the skillet. Add the coconut milk and cook, stirring frequently, for 2 minutes more, or until heated through and combined.

6. Serve the chops with the vegetables and gravy poured over the top.

Nutritional Information: Calories 416, Carbs: 10g, Fat: 24g, Fiber: 2g, Protein: 40g

Lemon-Garlic Pork Tenderloin with Radishes and Green Pepper

Serves: 8

Preparation time: 10 minutes

Cooking time: 8 hours

Ingredients

- 1-pound pork tenderloin
- ¼ cup olive oil
- 1 bunch of radishes (about 12), diced
- 1 green bell pepper, seeded and diced
- 1 cup bone broth
- ¾ cup Lemon-Garlic Dressing
- 4 lemon slices

Directions

1. Place the pork in a slow cooker and pour the olive oil over the top. Add the radishes and green bell pepper. Pour the broth and dressing over the top. Lay the lemon slices on top of the pork.
2. Cover and cook on low for 8 hours, or until the pork is very tender.

Nutritional Information: Calories 249, Carbs: 2g, Fat: 21g, Fiber: 0g, Protein: 13g

Citrus Pork Shoulder with Spicy Cilantro Ginger Sauce

Serves: 8

Preparation time: 10 minutes

Cooking time: 8 hours

Ingredients

- 8 cloves garlic, minced
- ¼ cup diced onions
- ¼ cup melted lard or avocado oil
- ¼ cup swerve confectioners
- 2 teaspoons ground black pepper
- 2 tablespoons fine sea salt
- 2 teaspoons smoked paprika
- Juice of 2 limes
- 4 drops orange oil
- 1 (6-pound) boneless pork shoulder

Spicy Cilantro Ginger Sauce

- ¼ cup chopped fresh cilantro
- 1 cup mayonnaise, homemade or store-bought
- ¼ cup lime juice
- 2 tablespoons chopped fresh chives
- 1 jalapeno pepper, seeded and coarsely chopped
- ½ teaspoon fine sea salt

For Garnish

- Lime wedges

Jenny Pale

- Freshly ground black pepper

Directions

1. Place the onions, garlic, melted lard, sweetener, salt, pepper, paprika, lime juice, and orange oil in a slow cooker. Stir to combine, then place the pork shoulder on top of the other ingredients. Turn the pork in the seasonings to coat it on all sides, then cover the slow cooker and cook on low for 8 hours or until the pork shreds easily.

2. Meanwhile, make the sauce: place all the ingredients for the sauce in a food processor and puree until very smooth. Set aside in the refrigerator until ready to serve

3. When the meat is done, shred it with 2 forks and toss the in the juices from the slow cooker.

4. Garnish with line wedges and freshly ground pepper.

5. Serves each portion of meat with 3 tablespoons of the sauce.

6. Store in an airtight container in the refrigerator for up to 3 days. To reheat, place the pork on a rimes baking sheet in a preheated 350F oven for 5 minutes or until warmed through.

Nutritional Information: Calories 712, Carbs: 3g, Fat: 59g, Fiber: 1g, Protein: 39g

Dry Rub Ribs

Serves: 8

Preparation time: 10 minutes

Cooking time: 8 hours

Ingredients

- 1 full rack baby back ribs, cut in half to fit in the pot
- 6 tablespoons olive oil
- 2 batches Red Pepper Dry Rub
- ½ cup water

Directions

1. Coat the ribs with the oil and then with the dry rub, and put them in a slow cooker with the water.
2. Cover and cook on low for 8 hours. Serve hot.

Nutritional Information: Calories 336, Carbs: 0g, Fat: 32g, Fiber: 0g, Protein: 12g

Bacon-Wrapped "Fried" Pickles

Serves: 12

Preparation time: 12 minutes

Cooking time: 25 Minutes

Ingredients

- 12 dill pickle spears
- 12 strips bacon

Directions

1. Preheat the oven to 400°F.
2. Wrap each pickle spear tightly with 1 piece of bacon.
3. Arrange the wrapped pickles on the baking sheet and bake for 25 minutes, or until the bacon is crispy.
4. Place on a wire rack to cool; the pickle juice and bacon fat make for a very hot

Nutritional Information: Calories 104, Carbs: 0g, Fat: 8g, Fiber: 0g, Protein: 7g

Stuffed Poblano Peppers

Serves: 5

Preparation time: 10 minutes

Cooking time: 40 Minutes

Ingredients

- 2 tablespoons olive oil, plus more for greasing the baking dish
- 1 pound ground pork
- 1 (4-ounce) can diced green chiles
- ½ cup tomato sauce
- 1 jalapeño pepper, chopped
- 1 tablespoon minced garlic
- 1 teaspoon dried basil
- 1 teaspoon salt
- 1 teaspoon freshly ground black pepper
- 5 poblano peppers

Directions

1. Preheat the oven to 400°F. Grease a 9-inch square baking dish.
2. In a large skillet, heat the olive oil over medium-high heat. Add the pork and begin to brown.
3. As the meat begins to brown, add the diced green chiles, tomato sauce, jalapeño, garlic, basil, salt, and pepper. Cook, stirring frequently, until the meat is browned, about 5 minutes.
4. Stuff each poblano pepper with the meat mixture, and arrange the stuffed peppers in the prepared baking dish. Bake in the preheated oven for 30 minutes, or until bubbling and browned on the top.

Nutritional Information: Calories 271, Carbs: 7g, Fat: 19g, Fiber: 2g, Protein: 18g

Shepherd's Pie

Serves: 10

Preparation time: 45 minutes

Cooking time: 8 hours

Ingredients

- 2 pounds ground sausage
- 1 (12-ounce) bag spinach
- 1 cup sliced mushrooms
- 1 onion, diced
- 1 cup bone broth
- ¼ cup coconut aminos
- 2 tablespoons minced garlic
- 1 recipe Cauliflower Mash, prepared but uncooked

Directions

1. In a slow cooker, combine the sausage, spinach, mushrooms, onion, broth, coconut aminos, and garlic.
2. Cover and cook on low for 7 hours.
3. Spread the Cauliflower Mash over the meat mixture. Cover and cook for an additional 30 minutes to 1 hour.
4. Serve hot.

Nutritional Information: Calories 476, Carbs: 6g, Fat: 40g, Fiber: 2g, Protein: 23g

Jenny Pale

Ground-Pork Skillet With Zucchini And Onion

Serves: 6

Preparation time: 10 minutes

Cooking time: 20 minutes

Ingredients

- 2 tablespoons olive oil
- 1 pound ground pork
- 1 large onion, diced
- 1 cup coconut milk
- 2 tablespoons minced garlic
- 1 teaspoon salt
- 1 teaspoon freshly ground black pepper
- 15 medium zucchini, spiralized

Directions

1. Heat the olive oil in a large skillet over medium-high heat. Add the pork and cook, stirring, until browned, about 5 minutes. Add the onion and cook, stirring frequently, until softened, about 5 more minutes.
2. Stir in the coconut milk, garlic, salt, and pepper. Reduce the heat to low and cook for about 10 more minutes, or until the sauce thickens.
3. Add the zucchini, toss to mix, and serve immediately.

Nutritional Information: Calories 329, Carbs: 5g, Fat: 29g, Fiber: 1g, Protein: 15g

Sausage Balls

Serves: 15 balls

Preparation time: 15 minutes

Cooking time: 25 minutes

Ingredients

- Oil, for greasing the baking sheet
- 1 pound loose breakfast sausage
- 2 tablespoons almond flour
- 1 tablespoon hot wing sauce (such as Frank's RedHot)
- 1 teaspoon cayenne

Directions

1. Preheat the oven to 350°F. Grease a large rimmed baking sheet.
2. In a medium bowl, thoroughly mix the breakfast sausage, almond flour, hot sauce, and cayenne. Form into bite-size balls and place on the greased baking sheet.
3. Bake for 25 minutes, or until browned and cooked through.

Nutritional Information: Calories 258, Carbs: 0g, Fat: 22g, Fiber: 0g, Protein: 15g

Chapter Eight: Desserts

No-Bake Haystack Cookies
Serves: 15 to 18 cookies

Preparation time: 10 minutes (plus 3hrs for chilling)

Ingredients

- 1 (8-ounce) container dairy-free cream cheese (such as Kite Hill)
- ¾ cup unsweetened shredded coconut
- ½ cup Swerve granular (or other granulated alternative sweetener)
- ¼ cup peanut butter
- 1 tablespoon cacao powder
- 1 tablespoon chia seeds

Directions

1. In a small microwave-safe bowl, melt the cream cheese in the microwave for 30 seconds. Whisk in the coconut, sweetener, peanut butter, cacao powder, and chia seeds.
2. On a baking sheet or plate, form the mixture into small domes, or "haystacks." Chill in the refrigerator for 3 hours (or until you've eaten them all).

Nutritional Information: Calories 172, Carbs: 5g, Fat: 16g, Fiber: 3g, Protein: 2g

Macadami Nut Butter Cups

Serves: 12 cups

Preparation time: 10 minutes (4 hours for chilling)

Ingredients

- Coconut oil, for greasing the pan
- 1 batch Macadamia Nut Butter
- ½ batch Chocolate Sauce

Directions

1. Grease a silicone muffin pan with coconut oil.
2. Pour the nut butter into the cups, dividing equally. Dampen your hands with cold water and use your fingertips to pat down and flatten the nut butter.
3. Freeze for at least 2 hours, or until hardened.
4. Pour the chocolate sauce over the chilled cups and freeze for at least another 2 hours, or until hardened. Serve straight from the freezer.

Nutritional Information: Calories 329, Carbs: 5g, Fat: 33g, Fiber: 1g, Protein: 3g

Chocolate Chip Skillet Cookie

Serves: 4

Preparation time: 10 minutes

Cook time: 25 minutes

Ingredients

- Coconut oil, for greasing the skillet
- 1 cup low-carb baking mix (I like Bob's Red Mill)
- ¾ cup Swerve granular (or another granulated alternative sweetener)
- ¾ cup cacao butter, melted
- 2 teaspoons vanilla extract
- ¼ cup dairy-free chocolate chips

Directions

1. Preheat the oven to 350°F. Grease a 7-inch cast iron skillet with coconut oil.
2. In a mixing bowl, stir together the low-carb baking mix and sweetener. Add the melted cacao butter and vanilla extract and mix until well combined. Fold in the chocolate chips.
3. Pour the mixture into the greased skillet and bake for 25 minutes

Nutritional Information: Calories 415, Carbs: 4g, Fat: 43g, Fiber: 1g, Protein: 3g

Chocolate Bacon With Pink Hi-Malayan Salt

Serves: 4

Preparation time: 10 minutes (2 hours for Freezing)

Cook time: 25 minutes

Ingredients

- 1 batch Perfect Bacon, cooled
- ½ batch Chocolate Sauce
- 1 tablespoon pink Himalayan salt

Directions

1. Arrange the bacon on a large rimmed baking sheet and drizzle the chocolate sauce over the top.
2. Sprinkle with the salt and freeze for at least 2 hours, or until hardened.
3. Serve chilled or store in a zip-top bag in the freezer

Nutritional Information: Calories 264, Carbs: 2g, Fat: 24g, Fiber: 0g, Protein: 10g

Conclusion

Thank you for purchasing a copy of this piece. I hoped it helped you enjoy a better life. I urge you to drop an honest review about the book to encourage others.

Printed in Great Britain
by Amazon